Holy Spirit

Dr. Cheryl Salem

Scripture quotations taken from the Amplified® Bible (AMPC), Copyright © 1954, 1958, 1962, 1964, 1965, 1987 by The Lockman Foundation Used by permission.

Holy Spirit

ISBN 9798421638414

Printed in United States of America

Copyright © 2022 by Salem Family Ministries

Salem Family Ministries
PO Box 1595
Cathedral City, CA 92235
www.salemfamilyministries.org

No part of this book may be reproduced or transmitted in any form or by any means, electronic or mechanical, including photocopying, recording, or by any information storage and retrieval system, without permission in writing from Salem Family Ministries.

Disclaimer: The views expressed in this book contain my personal opinions and experiences throughout my life and time spent in God's presence. I express them as my opinion and view only, and share them with you from my personal lifelong experience from my heart. I am only communicating what has worked for me personally, and what I have personally experienced with the Lord.

Table of Contents

Introduction to the Holy Spirit 5

Chapter One
Who is the Holy Spirit? 9

Chapter Two
Where does the Holy Spirit live? 17

Chapter Three
How do I Receive the Holy Spirit? 27

Chapter Four
What is the Work of the Holy Spirit? 39

Chapter Five
How do I Yield to the Holy Spirit? 49

Chapter Six
What are the Gifts of the Holy Spirit? 57

Chapter Seven
What is the Fruit of the Holy Spirit? 69

Chapter Eight
The Correlation Between the Fruit
and the Gifts of the Holy Spirit 81

Chapter Nine
Jesus' Relationship with the Holy Spirit 91

Chapter Ten
The Nature of the Spirit of God is Fire 103

Chapter Eleven
Three Baptisms: Water, Holy Spirit, and Fire .. 121

Chapter Twelve
The Holy Spirit Speaks and Sings through You   137

Chapter Thirteen
The Hierarchy of the Kingdom of God 143

Chapter Fourteen
How to be Led by Holy Spirit 153

Chapter Fifteen
The Seven-fold Spirits of God 161

Chapter Sixteen
Holy Spirit is our Witness in
Heaven and on Earth 167

Introduction

Who is the Holy Spirit? Let me introduce you! Holy Spirit this is my friend. I believe I heard the Holy Spirit say, "I'm glad to meet you." My friend, I would like to introduce you to Holy Spirit. I hope you are saying right this moment that you are glad to meet Him! Through this book I plan to not only introduce you to Holy Spirit but also help you become intimately acquainted, and personally intertwined with Him.

God is triune, and we are made in His image as triune beings. The biggest difference is our triune spirit, soul, and body has one of the three that must conquer the other two at all times. Our spirit man must lead, and conquer our soul and body. With our triune God, they are truly three in one. They are all God, manifesting in different forms at different times but always in harmony and unity and never in any conflict with each other. There is definite order, rank, and authority as you will see as you read this book, and read God's word.

God is Father, Son, and Holy Spirit. He has three personas or manifestations. When we read about Jesus in the New Testament, He speaks of representing His Father at all times. When He was preparing His disciples for His departure from the earth, He taught them that the Holy Spirit would come and take His place.

He taught that the Holy Spirit would represent Him at all times. Jesus told His disciples in John 14:16 that He would ask the Father, and the Father would give us another Comforter, Counselor, Helper, Intercessor, Advocate, Strengthener, and Standby, the Holy Spirit. Jesus taught the disciples that the Holy Spirit would remain with us forever.

Just from this one verse it is easy to see how complex the Holy Spirit is in His being. There are many verses describing the

Holy Spirit, but in this one verse we can see the multifaceted dimension of who this one of the Godhead is to us and for us.

Who is the Holy Spirit? He is the third mentioned of the Godhead, and the representative of Jesus in the New Testament. In the Old Testament the Spirit of God, the Holy Spirit, was the representative of Father God. In the governmental order of heaven, He is the Godhead over worship.

The topic of the Holy Spirit is so vast there is no way to cover all of Who He is in a book, but we can study and prepare ourselves to house Him from this day forth. To know the Holy Spirit is to know Father and Son. We must learn more about Who He is and what our purpose is concerning the Holy Spirit on the earth through us. He came to live in us. He came to be housed in flesh, your flesh and mine.

Will you let Him move into your very being and never leave? This is His desire, to be one with you.

In this book we will discuss how the Holy Spirit manifests through people, and how to yield to His presence. We will talk about the correlation between the fruit of the Holy Spirit and the gifts of the Holy Spirit in operation.

I want to introduce you to the Holy Spirit in a more intimate and personal way through these pages in hopes that once you are finished with this study you will be 'wall to wall' covered with His presence and power.

The Holy Spirit is the power of God in operation. He is the voice of the triune God on the earth. He is the fire, the water, and the shaking earthquake; He is the Spirit hovering over everything and He is the frequency vibration of creation. He is the still small voice and the nudging hand of direction. He longs for you. Do you long for Him? You should; He is the very life force and GPS on your road to eternity.

He has many names and all describe a portion of Who He is. He is Wisdom. He is the Spirit of Truth. He is the sound of heaven and the fire tongue! The more you study about Holy Spirit the more you realize He is infinite, just like Father God. His definitions are infinite too.

He is . . . well, whatever it is you need, He is that too. He is the very expression of your healing, your breakthrough, and your deliverance. Does He sound like Jesus to you? Well, He should! Father sent Him to represent Jesus, to take His place on earth for us, and in us!

Isaiah 11:2 describes the seven-fold Spirit in detail. He is the Spirit of holy. He is the Spirit of wisdom. He is the Spirit of understanding. He is the Spirit of counsel. He is the Spirit of might. He is the Spirit of knowledge. He is the Spirit of the reverential and obedient fear of the Lord. We will discuss this further within the pages ahead.

This will be a journey of His presence. This will be the most intimate of times with the very Lover of your soul. He will truly make you whole if you let Him.

In this book we will discuss Who the Holy Spirit is, where He lives, when He came to earth, and many other topics all on the Holy Spirit. My prayer for you is by the time we complete this journey together you will be so filled to overflowing with the Holy Spirit that you will never be the same ever again! Let's walk these pages together. Let me introduce you and show you, and what do you do? Well, you can completely and totally experience His presence from now through eternity.

Chapter One
Who is the Holy Spirit?

It has taken me a lifetime to realize the Holy Spirit has been with me since I was a very little girl. I grew up in a Southern Mississippi Christian home. We went to church three times a week, every week, and more if there was something special happening. In the summer time we went all week, morning and evening for 'Summer Revival.' My family is very musical so we sang in church. I started playing the piano in church almost before I can remember. We led the congregational singing, and we sang 'specials' almost every service too.

Sometimes when you grow up like I did, and many people grew up just like me, you know that you love the Lord, but you don't really 'know' Him. All my life I felt His presence with me, even when I didn't realize it was 'His presence,' I still knew it was the Lord.

He has led me, kept me, protected me, and even been with me in the midst of some pretty horrible experiences. He never left me. He never stood on the finish line and said, "When you come out of this mess, I will be waiting for you." Nope, He walked every step of some horrific and traumatic experiences. I now realize how many times He led me to turn this way, go that way, run to the woods, walk out to the church, and so on. He would simply give me an idea or thought that I considered at the time to be my own mind, but now I realize it was His constant companionship, and gentle leading even as a very small young girl.

I spent many an afternoon down in the woods, in the holler, on a tree stump, writing songs and singing at the top of my lungs, or preaching and teaching the little creatures that were sure to be there! I always thought that was just 'life in the country,' but now I realize that is 'life with the Holy Spirit.'

He is still with me even as I type these words for you to read. He never leaves me. When I am happy and smiling and singing and filled with joy, He is with me. When I am grumpy and sad, and whiny, and discouraged, He is with me.

Who is the Holy Spirit, and why is He always with me? He is the presence of Almighty God, and He wants to be with me. He wants to be housed by me. All my life I have hungered for more of God.

I have cried and searched, and read my Bible and prayed. My hunger for my God brought His Holy Spirit to be with me, guiding me on the right paths, and helping me make the right choices to find Him early in my life.

Jesus said it like this.

Blessed and fortunate and happy and spiritually prosperous (in that state in which the born-again child of God enjoys His favor and salvation) are those who hunger and thirst for righteousness (uprightness and right standing with God), for they shall be completely satisfied! Matthew 5:6

Wait and listen, everyone who is thirsty! Come to the waters; and he who has no money, come, buy and eat! Yes, come, buy [priceless, spiritual] wine and milk without money and without price [simply for the self-surrender that accepts the blessing]. Why do you spend your money for that which is not bread, and your earnings for what does not satisfy? Hearken diligently to Me, and eat what is good, and let your soul delight itself in fatness [the profuseness of spiritual joy]. Isaiah 55:1-2

Who is the Holy Spirit? He is the one who makes you hungry and then satisfies you. He is the one who makes you thirsty and then delights to give you plenty to quench your thirst!

The Holy Spirit is the expression of God. The Holy Spirit is God in manifestation. The Holy Spirit represents Jesus on the earth to all of us who love Him and are called according to His name.

Who is the Holy Spirit? When God said, 'Let there be light,' the Holy Spirit was there hovering over the earth, brooding over it, like a mother hen giving birth to everything Father God said. He said it, and Holy Spirit would cause it to come forth.

In the beginning was the Word, the sound wave, the creative force and nature of God through sound waves. Father said it, 'Let there be Light!' Jesus is the light of the world. Father spoke Jesus into earth's existence in the very beginning. Before man was ever created, God knew we would fall and need a Savior. Father made provision for our redemption before we ever fell.

Oh, what a Father He is! His only Son, wrapped Himself in flesh for us, then sent the very expression of God, the Holy Spirit to take His place. Just as Jesus wrapped Himself in flesh, He made a way for the Holy Spirit to be wrapped in us! For thousands of years, the Holy Spirit was on the earth, and 'with men' but 2000 plus years ago, He was sent to the earth to not only be with humanity but to ultimately be within humanity. He became the sound of heaven to the earth, the fire power for all mankind to have, to be changed forever, baptized in the Holy Ghost and His fire, changing our tongues from earth speaking to heaven speaking!

The Holy Spirit has many names and many expressions. He is the Spirit of God. He is Jesus' representative on the earth after Christ's ascension. He is Shekinah, God's visible presence as man looks upon God's glory manifested.

Then the cloud [the Shekinah, God's visible presence] covered the Tent of Meeting, and the glory of the Lord filled the tabernacle! Exodus 40:34

Holy Spirit is Sanctifier for humanity.

There I will meet with the Israelites, and the Tent of Meeting shall be sanctified by My glory [the Shekinah, God's visible presence]. Exodus 29:43

He is the cloud filling the inner court of the temple.

Now the cherubim stood on the south side of the house when the man went in; and the cloud [the Shekinah] filled the inner court. Ezekiel 10:3

Holy Spirit is the glory of God that moves within the temple and stands.

Then the glory of the Lord [the Shekinah, cloud] went forth from above the threshold of the temple and stood over the cherubim. Ezekiel 10:18

When anointed leadership blesses the people the glory of the Lord comes and appears to all the people.

Moses and Aaron went into the Tent of Meeting, and when they came out they blessed the people, and the glory of the Lord [the Shekinah cloud] appeared to all the people [as promised]. Leviticus 9:23

Nations can be blessed with God's presence and glory.

For they are Israelites, and to them belong God's adoption [as a nation] and the glorious Presence (Shekinah). With them were the special covenants made, to them was the Law given. To them [the temple] worship was revealed and [God's own] promises announced. Romans 9:4

I could go on and on and show you hundreds of scriptures in reference to the manifested presence of God. Suffice it to say we will spend all of eternity getting to know Who is the Holy Spirit. As one of the Godhead, the feminine expression of the Godhead according to Strongs number 3519, is 'kabod' pronounced kaw-bode. It is defined as properly weight; but only figuratively in a good (sense) splendor or copiousness - glorious, glory, honor and honorable. That word comes from the Hebrew word 'kabad' pronounced kaw-bade. It is the Strong's number 3513.

In the scripture reference in Romans 9:4 it is translated from the Strongs number 1391 which means 'doxa'. Defined from the base of Strongs number 1380; glory (as very apparent) in a wide application (literally or figuratively objectively or subjectively): - dignity, glory (ious), honor, praise, worship.

When God's presence is manifested, one cannot stop themselves from praising and worshiping the one true God! His presence draws our worship! He calls us, pursues us, and woos us. As the bride of Christ, God's presence draws us to Himself, and we can't stop our worship from flowing out of us! If you are not compelled to worship God when His presence is manifesting, you should ask yourself do you know Him? Those who know Him will worship Him in Spirit and Truth spontaneously!

He is the cloud by day and the fire by night. He is the divine connection between Father and humanity on the earth today. I will go into much further detail throughout every chapter of truly 'who' is Holy Spirit! He is infinite, ever expanding within us as we run after His presence!

Who is the Holy Spirit? He first is written of in Genesis 1:2, *And the earth was without form, and void; and darkness was upon the face of the deep. And the Spirit of God moved upon the face of the waters.*

The Spirit of God is the Strongs number 7307, Ruach, pronounced 'roo-akh'. Defined as wind; by resemblance {breath} that {is} a sensible (or even violent) exhalation; figuratively {life} anger unsubstantiality; by extension a region of the sky; by resemblance {spirit} but only of a rational being (including its expression and functions). The very first reference to the Spirit of God is the actual breath of God.

For me personally, who is Holy Spirit? He's closer than my own breath. He comforts me when it is impossible to soothe my soul. He touches me when I am seemingly untouchable. He breaks through the thickest and highest walls of my heart. He speaks to me, and I can hear Him when it seems not another soul can get through to me. He explains what is unexplainable. He heals what is not healable. He's for me when I feel like the entire world is against me. Who is Holy Spirit?

I will spend eternity knowing God's presence more and more, but having Him with me in my earth experience is truly beyond expression and completely priceless for me. He is most valuable of all values. I never want to live one moment without Him. Father, take not Your Holy Spirit from me, ever please, for I would imagine I would die within minutes of His departure from a broken heart. He is the Lover of my soul, the One who makes me whole.

It seems impossible for me to stop giving you more and more information about who is the Holy Spirit so I will simply stop this chapter and move on to the next!

Chapter Two
Where does the Holy Spirit live?

He waits for you in your secret place. This is your secret prayer place, and He has waited for you a very long time. Will you continue to keep Him waiting, or will you simply go in and be with Him? That is up to you. I will show you how, but ultimately, it's your choice whether you abandon your flesh and join Him, spirit to Spirit.

But you, when you pray, go into your room, and when you have shut your door, pray to your Father who is in the secret place; and your Father who sees in secret will reward you openly.
Matthew 6:6 NKJV

Do you see here that you are going inside yourself to meet in a secret place with Father? He is waiting for you; He waits as the One who lives inside you. The Holy Spirit was sent to the earth to move inside your very being, to be housed in your flesh! The Holy Spirit, once you give Him permission to move in, will take up residency within you!

How does the Holy Spirit get inside my flesh? How does He

move into my being? Let's look at the very first time we see Holy Spirit move into a human person's flesh.

It started with a promise from Jesus.

And I will ask the Father, and He will give you another Comforter (Counselor, Helper, Intercessor, Advocate, Strengthener, and Standby), that He may remain with you forever-the Spirit of Truth, Whom the world cannot receive (welcome, take to its heart), because it does not see Him or know and recognize Him. But you know and recognize Him, for He lives with you [constantly] and will be in you.
John 14:16-17

Jesus had more to say about Holy Spirit.

But the Comforter (Counselor, Helper, Intercessor, Advocate, Strengthener, Standby), the Holy Spirit, Whom the Father will send in My name [in My place, to represent Me and act on My behalf], He will teach you all things. And He will cause you to recall (will remind you of, bring to your remembrance) everything I have told you. Peace I leave with you; My [own] peace I now give and bequeath to you. Not as the world gives do I give to you. Do not let your hearts be troubled, neither let them be afraid. [Stop allowing yourselves to be agitated and disturbed; and do not permit yourselves to be fearful and intimidated and cowardly and unsettled.] John 14:26-27

Jesus simply and plainly introduced His disciples to the Holy Spirit in those few verses. He explained to them what was about to happen. He explained to them Who the Holy Spirit is to them personally and then Jesus gave them, literally willed them, the peace of the Holy Spirit Who was dwelling in Jesus, to be theirs if they would only receive Him.

He warned them to protect their hearts and discipline it to the point of not letting their hearts be troubled. 'Don't let your heart be troubled,' Jesus said. Don't give it permission to be troubled. Don't be afraid! Control your fear! All of this was said to Jesus' disciples in explanation of what they could expect once they had received the peace of the Holy Spirit within them. It would be their responsibility from that point on to never be troubled in their hearts or allow fear to ever make them afraid again!

So the promise of Holy Spirit was given, but when did Holy Spirit come to the earth?

You shall receive power when the Holy Spirit comes upon you. Acts 1:8

When I was 17 years old, I went to a meeting held by Brother Kenneth E. Hagin in Jackson, MS. It is a very long story and is covered in great detail in my very first book over 40 years ago titled, "A Bright Shining Place-The Story of a Miracle."

I was a senior in High School and had been invited to this Monday night, October 21, 1974, service in an old hotel in Jackson. We drove down packed into a car, to hear this man speak on faith. Everyone else knew who Brother Hagin was except me. I had no idea that he was a famous preacher on faith.

I had been told that he would pray for the sick and that maybe the Lord would touch me and heal my almost two-inch shorter left leg. We arrived early enough to get seats really close to the front, and since I was most definitely the youngest and most certainly the newest to this group, I had to sit on the very inside of the seats about mid-way down the row. The service was wonderful. The music and worship were powerful and the word preached was like nothing I had ever heard before. I was enthralled with every word Brother Hagin said.

I had already spent six weeks reading my Bible, studying to see what I really believe about healing, and my healing specifically. I knew that God wanted to heal me; I knew that God was going to heal me that very evening. I had never been in any kind of meeting like this before but I felt very much 'at home.'

I waited. I waited for my time to be healed. I waited for Brother Hagin to ask me to come forward to the altar. I had no idea how or when it would happen, but I knew that it would. I had already decided that it would. I knew it in my knower. The Holy Spirit was obviously helping guide me even in my own spirit and soul. I was ready to be healed. I was ready to receive.

Finally, Brother Hagin gave the invitation for those who needed healing to come to the altar, and I jumped up and made my way quickly across all the knees of everyone that I had come with and stood front and center! I was ready! I looked around, and all these other people kept coming and coming. I said to the Lord, "Father, all these folks are coming but this is my miracle. This is my healing. They can come if they want to. You can heal them if You want to, but tonight this is my miracle."

I made a declaration. I wasn't being selfish. I was just stating that all these other people's needs were not going to distract me from the weeks I had spent studying and working out my belief system. I had come for my miracle, and I most certainly was not leaving without it.

It came. As I stood there waiting for Brother Hagin to get to me, I decided to just be with my Father. I think that is probably when I really began to discover the true secret place within me. I turned loose of the controls and I simply said, "Lord, give me anything and everything You want me to have."

That settled it completely. He wanted me to have my miracle. Within a few seconds my left leg grew out to be the same length as my right leg. I had back issues, also, from the car accident that had left me crippled in my leg, and my back was healed instantly also. I had ulcers in my stomach, and they were healed immediately.

I lifted my hands, which I had never done before, and began to praise God and thank Him and give Him glory for healing me. All of a sudden, I went right out of English into the most beautiful language I had ever heard before! I was amazed that out of this southern twanging speaking girl, this glorious language was pouring out!

I couldn't stop it. I didn't want to stop it! It was flowing and flowing and coming up out of my belly! My head was screaming, "What are you doing!?" But it was too late to stop! Joy had overtaken me, and rivers of living water were gushing from my being, using my vocal cords as they came forth!

I had no idea what was happening but I was totally at peace. I loved it! I got up off the floor and made my way back to my seat, trying out my perfectly proportioned two legs the same length, smiling, crying, and weeping in this wonderful foreign language.

What almost no one in the whole world knew was getting to go to college was a huge thing for me! But I had recently been told that I didn't have one of the prerequisites needed to enter Mississippi State University, a foreign language. I was a senior at Weir High School. There were 35 in my graduating class. There was no foreign language offered at my school! A few weeks earlier I had taken it to the Lord with a simple "I trust You to work this out for me" prayer.

So as I lay there on the floor at the altar giving God all the glory for the miracle He had just performed in my body, as I began to praise Him in a foreign tongue, my mind said a big 'Thank You, Father' for the foreign language I will need to complete my prerequisites for college! Yep, that is exactly what I was thinking!

The evening went on, and I finally figured out that the Holy Spirit had come upon me, and I was filled to overflowing with rivers of living water. I had been baptized in the Holy Ghost.

Holy Spirit moves into our being, literally inside of us, when He is invited. I yielded myself to the will of Father when I said, "Give me anything and everything You want me to have." The openness of that yielding allowed Father to give me the Holy Spirit. Ultimately, I had to yield my will to His will, and Holy Spirit went from being 'with me' to being 'in me.'

I figured out that out of my belly a sound from heaven filled my being for the rest of my eternal life! That was my first time to be filled with the power of the Holy Ghost and to speak in other tongues, but it was not the first time the Holy Spirit had spoken through a human!

And when the day of Pentecost had fully come, they were all assembled together in one place, when suddenly there came a sound from heaven like the rushing of a violent tempest blast, and it filled the whole house in which they were sitting. And there appeared to them tongues resembling fire, which were separated and distributed and which settled on each one of them. And they were all filled (diffused throughout their souls) with the Holy Spirit and began to speak in other (different, foreign) languages (tongues), as the Spirit kept giving them clear and loud expression [in each tongue in appropriate words]. Acts 2:1-4

Jesus promised us the Holy Spirit. He promised us power when the Holy Spirit comes upon us. He said Father would send the Holy Spirit to be with us as Jesus' representative. And then Jesus was crucified, dead and in the tomb for three days. Then He rose from the dead! Then He disappeared, and they had no idea where He went. He went to Father. Then He came back, and He stayed around, coming and going, walking through walls, and doing what can be done in a glorified flesh body!

Yes, Jesus is still housed in flesh. It's glorified flesh so it can walk through walls and stuff like that but it's still flesh! For all of eternity, Jesus shed His Godhead body to wear our flesh body. FOR ALL OF ETERNITY! It's one thing to sacrifice thirty-three years of eternal Godhead body to wear humanity, but to shed eternal Godhead body forever? Yes, that's what Jesus did for us.

He hung around with His people for another forty days with the last words to them was to tarry in Jerusalem until Father sends the Holy Spirit. Another ten days passed, and the wonderful holiday weekend of Pentecost came! While they were all still reeling from Jesus ascending in the clouds and leaving them here on earth, they gathered for Pentecost (holiday) weekend.

There were hundreds of followers of Jesus during the time of His ascension, but ten days later in the upper room those hundreds had dwindled down to one hundred and twenty people. We don't know a lot about how they were feeling, or what they were thinking. We know one thing about them. They were all in one accord. They were all in agreement. They were waiting for Holy Spirit to be sent by Father God. They waited, when others would not wait. They were in agreement which brings the very Spirit of God in our midst.

Again I say to you that if two believers on earth agree [that is, are of one mind, in harmony] about anything that they ask [within the will of God] it will be done for them by My Father in heaven. For where two or three are gathered in My name [meeting together as My followers] I am there among them.
Matthew 18:19-20

Jesus had already taught them about agreement and how it is a legal summons to the Holy Spirit. You might say that is not what He said because Jesus said that He would be there among them when they gathered in agreement. Yes, that's true. But Jesus also taught them in John fourteen that He was leaving the earth and that He would pray to Father, and Father would send the Holy Spirit to represent Jesus, to take His place on the earth with them.

I can just imagine the disciples having long discussions about how they could bring this about to receive the representative of Jesus Christ. It was fifty days after His crucifixion and resurrection. It was a legal Jewish holiday, Pentecost, where the Jews gathered together to celebrate the giving of the Word through Moses to His people. God gave the Ten Commandments to Moses on the same weekend He was about to give the Holy Spirit to the earth. The Word and the Spirit given to the earth was about to become the very celebration of Pentecost for the rest of time.

They gathered together. They waited. I imagine they worshiped and sang and prayed. I imagine they discussed at length their love for Jesus and their thankfulness of His coming to earth to save them. They probably ate some meals and drank some coffee too. (Well, that's what I would have been drinking while I waited!).

Maybe they were fasting. Who knows the details, but we know the outcome. When the Day of Pentecost had fully come, they were all in agreement, not a dispute among them; everyone was in one accord.

Then suddenly the room was filled with the sound of heaven! The sound of heaven filled the whole room, and it was loud! Frequencies and sounds that only heaven can make came swooping in like a big old wind storm! Boom! They were all filled with the Holy Spirit and began to speak in tongues!

The sound of heaven had filled the room, then filled the people as they received the Holy Spirit for Whom they had been waiting. He was given by Father to mankind, and they were the first to receive Holy Spirit! They spoke in foreign languages, loud and clear; they must have been praising God in these foreign languages.

Do you not know that your body is the temple (the very sanctuary) of the Holy Spirit Who lives within you, Whom you have received [as a Gift] from God? You are not your own.
1 Corinthians 6:19

Where does the Holy Spirit live? Since the very day of Pentecost fully coming, He lives on the earth. He is housed in flesh inside human bodies. Our bodies can become His temple!

He wants to live inside you, but it's your choice. It always has been, and it always will be. He will never move into your being until you truly invite Him without reservation. Holy Spirit is a gentleman and will only live where He is welcomed. You must fully yield your will to His will and as Jesus promised in John fourteen, then the Holy Spirit will move from being with you, to being in you!

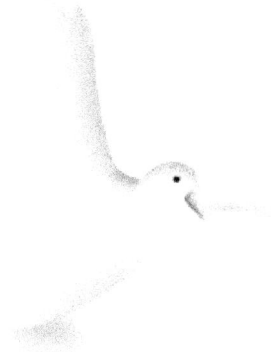

Chapter Three
How do I Receive the Holy Spirit?

I shared with you how I received the Holy Spirit at Kenneth Hagin's service on a Monday night, at the old Heidelberg Hotel in Jackson, MS. I wasn't even really aware of Who the Holy Spirit is. I mean I grew up in a precious Methodist Church, Salem Methodist Church, to be exact. I knew the Holy Spirit from the Apostles' Creed we confessed regularly.

I believe in God, the Father Almighty,
maker of heaven and earth;
And in Jesus Christ His only Son, our Lord;
Who was conceived by the Holy Spirit,
born of the Virgin Mary,
suffered under Pontius Pilate,
was crucified, dead, and buried;
the third day He rose from the dead;
He ascended into heaven,
and sits at the right hand
of God the Father Almighty;
from thence He shall come to judge

> the quick and the dead.
> I believe in the Holy Spirit,
> the communion of the saints,
> the forgiveness of sins,
> the resurrection of the body,
> and the life everlasting,
> Amen.

I was introduced to the name of the third Godhead through this confession each week as I grew up in our little Methodist church. By the time I was 13 years old, our little congregation was pulling away from the United Methodist organization and formed an Independant Methodist Church, also named, Salem Independant Methodist Church. We no longer recited the Apostle's Creed, but I had said it so many times I had the confession in my heart. I believe in the Holy Spirit. I believe in the Holy Spirit. I believe in the Holy Spirit.

Every time I made that confession as a little girl my heart opened up more and more to know whom I believe. I was hungry for more of God from such a young age I can't even remember when the hunger began! I was parched with thirst to drink from a well of living water that would burst forth from my being. But I didn't know at the time what or who I was so hungry and thirsty for; but the hunger and thirst was so evident in my being that I was on a search for a lifetime that was beyond this earthly realm of living and being.

I knew it; I just couldn't verbalize it yet. As I grew more and more in love with Jesus I began to hunger for more of His presence. I would find times to be alone, whether in my room or in the woods, just so I could talk to Jesus unreservedly. Now I know I was hungering for the One of the Godhead Who was sent to take Jesus' place with me on earth, the Holy Spirit.

Jesus taught His disciples in John chapter fourteen that He

would ask Father, and Father would send His representative, the Holy Spirit, to be with anyone who would receive Him, accept Him, and invite Him to live inside of their very being.

How do you receive the Holy Spirit? You ask Him to come and live inside of your being. You house the Holy Spirit inside your body, your soul, and in the depth of your spirit man.

Recently I was boiling some eggs to prepare them for dinner. As I was pouring off the hot water, putting them in ice cold water, and cracking the shell, the Holy Spirit began to speak to me. He said that an egg is very similar to humanity in that it is triune. I stopped cracking the eggs and simply said, "What?"

The Holy Spirit said it again. An egg is very similar to a triune human. The outer shell is like the physical flesh body. The white of the egg is like the soul, and the center yellow of the egg is like the spirit of a human being.

He said to walk fully spirit led and to be called sons and daughters of the Lord one must be fully spirit led and not controlled by either their soul (mind, will and emotions), or their flesh bodies. He said to be fully spirit led, one must conquer the body and soul and bring them under subjection to the spirit man within.

He went on to show me the correlation between the three levels of the temple as well. Our bodies are like the outer court, our souls are like the inner court, and our spirits are the Holy of Holies within our beings.

I was trying to peel the shell off the egg, and I got in too big of a hurry with one. It hadn't had enough time to soak in the cold water and bring separation between the shell and the white of the egg. The Holy Spirit began to speak to me about this process. He said, "You are a spirit. You have a soul, and you are housed in a body. You must be spirit led to be fully walking in the kingdom of heaven. To have your spirit lead, your soul and body must be broken and come under full control of the Holy Spirit. When Father is using Me to break your soul and body it is much easier when you are soaking in the Water of the Word, which helps bring separation between your body (flesh) and your soul."

I am still trying to peel the eggs while I listen to the Holy Spirit. I had hurried a few of the eggs in peeling them and had scarred the white portion on a few of them. The other eggs had more time to sit in the water with their shells cracked, and the shells had peeled off easily leaving no visible marks on the white of the egg.

All of a sudden, I saw the revelation. God wants to break our flesh and soul from trying to lead our lives. He wants us to be fully submitted to the Spirit of God, the Holy Spirit, who lives inside our spirits when we invite Him.

If we resist the process then we can be hurt, scarred more, from our resistance. If we soak ourselves continually in the Word of God (water) our bodies will more easily turn loose of its grip to want to be in control. Our souls are the inner court, the cushion, so to speak, between our bodies and our spirits. We can easily get hung up in the soul realm because of the resistance in the breaking of the body, to the point we wind up being fully controlled by our thinking and our feelings.

Thinking and feeling can keep you in a prison all its own. Your soul wanting to be in control can cause you to be in turmoil and have no peace your entire life. If you have been wounded by someone early in your life, or trust has been broken by another person, we may begin to walk through life as the 'walking wounded.'

Until we allow the Holy Spirit to lead us completely, we may be tormented in either our flesh (body) or our soul (mind, will, emotions). Some people are tormented in both these realms because they completely resist allowing Holy Spirit to lead them.

How do I receive the Holy Spirit? I yield my flesh, mind, will, emotions to Him. I fully trust Him to never hurt me, never leave me, and never forsake me. He promised that He would always be with us but only if we allow Him.

If you truly want to receive the Holy Spirit then you must first receive Jesus as your Lord and Savior. Most people who pray the sinner's prayer, or walk the aisle of a church in response to an altar call, give Jesus His position as Savior, but not Lord. Without His lordship one may not truly be saved, but rather have had a response to conviction without a true conversion.

Conversion means my old man died, passed away, and is buried. My old man is gone forever. This can only happen when Jesus not only becomes my Savior, but He is my Lord. His lordship over me means I have fully yielded my future to His will. He is my Lord. I confess it; I believe it. I allow Him this position in my life forever from that moment forward. He is Lord of my life, not just Savior. When Jesus is Lord of your life, then man cannot lord over you; debt cannot lord over you; fear cannot lord over you. He will not share His lordship with another.

Because if you acknowledge and confess with your lips that Jesus is Lord and in your heart believe (adhere to, trust in, and rely on the truth) that God raised Him from the dead, you will be saved. Romans 10:9

For what we preach is not ourselves but Jesus Christ as Lord, and ourselves [merely] as your servants (slaves) for Jesus' sake. 2 Corinthians 4:5

Jesus must become Lord of your life! He must be in full control of you! That's up to you. You can't pray that He will be Lord; you must yield your own will to accept Him as Lord. Then you can live the rest of your life, day by day, yielding your will to His will. What a wonderful journey!

In Acts chapter nineteen we see Paul on a journey. Paul had a full conversion and completely yielded his life to Jesus Christ as Lord. He was on a journey through the upper inland districts of Corinth and came down to Ephesus. In Ephesus Paul found some people who had given their hearts and lives to Jesus. I'm sure he was delighted to find other believers! He was looking for them, so he was going to find them! Whatever you are looking for in this life journey, you will always find it.

If you are not looking for the Holy Spirit, you will never find Him. If you are not looking for Jesus, you will never find Him. If you are not looking for Healer, Deliverer, Waymaker, you will never find Him. Whatever you are looking for, or whomever you are looking for, that and only that, will you find.

If you are looking for trouble, you will always find it. If you are looking for torment, fear, anxiety, panic, fatigue, exhaustion, being overwhelmed, guess what? You will always find what you are looking for! Paul was looking for fellow believers, and he found them!

He greeted them in verse two with these words. The very first words from Paul's mouth were what was in the forefront of his spirit.

And he asked them, Did you receive the Holy Spirit when you believed [on Jesus as the Christ]? And they said, No, we have not even heard that there is a Holy Spirit. Acts 19:12

You have to realize that Paul was freshly converted and was in a full conversion experience. He obviously had been baptized in the Holy Ghost and was going on his journey looking for others to introduce not only Jesus Christ as Lord to them, but also, he was wanting to see people baptized in the Holy Spirit as well! He continued on in conversation with them in the next few verses, preparing them for the baptism of the Holy Spirit that was about to come upon them!

Paul knew that the Holy Spirit had been given to the earth for all who had accepted Jesus Christ as Lord and Savior. He also knew that receiving the Holy Spirit was a separate experience from one's salvation conversion, and that each believer had to receive the Holy Spirit just as they had chosen to receive Jesus as the Christ. He presented it that way to the group in Ephesus as you will see in the verses following.

And he asked, Into what [baptism] then were you baptized? They said, into John's baptism. And Paul said, John baptized with the baptism of repentance, continually telling the people that they should believe in the One Who was to come after him, that is, in Jesus [having a conviction full of joyful trust that He is Christ, the Messiah, and being obedient to Him]. On hearing this they were baptized [again, this time] in the name of the Lord Jesus. And as Paul laid his hands upon them, the Holy Spirit came on them; and they spoke in [foreign, unknown] tongues (languages) and prophesied. There were about twelve of them in all. Acts 19:3-7

How do you receive the Holy Spirit? First, you must receive Jesus Christ as your Lord and Savior. Then you must decide that you also want to receive the Holy Spirit and accept His full control of your being. You must yield your body, and your soul to the power and control of the Holy Spirit, and when you truly receive Him, YOU WILL PRAY, SPEAK, AND WORSHIP IN ANOTHER LANGUAGE.

It is so easily seen in Acts 2:1-4. Let me show it to you again. Notice what the people were doing. Notice what the one hundred and twenty people were doing to put themselves in position to receive the Holy Spirit. They were assembled, not gathered together. They were put together in one accord, as one body in unison and unity. They were looking for the Holy Spirit to be given. They were setting themselves in position to receive.

And when the day of Pentecost had fully come, they were all assembled together in one place, when suddenly there came a sound from heaven like the rushing of a violent tempest blast, and it filled the whole house in which they were sitting. And there appeared to them tongues resembling fire, which were separated and distributed and which settled on each one of them. And they were all filled (diffused throughout their souls) with the Holy Spirit and began to speak in other (different, foreign) languages (tongues), as the Spirit kept giving them clear and loud expression [in each tongue in appropriate words]. Acts 2:1-4

Do you see what they were doing? They were assembled together!

Do not forsake the assembling of ourselves together, as is the manner of some, but exhorting one another, and so much the more as you see the Day approaching. Hebrews 10:25 (NKJV)

Let's look at that verse in the AMPC translation.

Not forsaking or neglecting to assemble together [as

believers], as is the habit of some people, but admonishing (warning, urging, and encouraging) one another, and all the more faithfully as you see the day approaching.

Notice the word 'assemble.' It is used to describe how the people were together in Acts chapter two. They were not just gathered in the upper room, but all one hundred and twenty of them were assembled.

My husband loves the Corvette car, especially the 1958 Corvette. He was born in 1958 so I assume that is why he loves that particular body style the most. I could gather every part of a 1958 Corvette and put it all in our garage. But it would not be the 1958 Corvette. It would simply be all the parts to a 1958 Corvette.

It would take hours and hours, weeks and weeks, months and months, and quite possibly, years to make all those parts that I gathered together into the 1958 Corvette car that he would prize so very much. Gathering is one thing, and most people in our society are very good at it. But assembling is a whole new level that we seldom see accomplished anymore. Assembling takes time, effort, hard work and much patience.

They were assembled in the upper room. They were put together; all the one hundred and twenty parts were assembled to become one whole body of believers. We are so concerned about 'self' in our society that we seldom ever actually assemble ourselves with any group. It is a dying process, a laying down of one's self to become a part of a whole body. As long as you're coming to church and it is about what you can 'get' from that body, or even from that service, then you will never be assembled. Assembled means you operate in your gift for the good of the whole body.

Assembling will never be about 'getting' but about 'giving' of yourself to benefit the work of the ministry, the work of the Lord for the good of the whole body. In the upper room they were assembled. There is not one mention of a name of who was gathered. We assume from later scriptures who was there from the disciples, but in Acts chapter two in the first few verses when we get to witness the first time Father sent Holy Spirit to take Jesus' place, to represent Jesus from that point to the very end of humanity, no human names are mentioned.

The giving of the Holy Spirit was for humanity to simply assemble together, and then receive the sound frequency given from heaven to earth. It was the time for humanity to receive the very Ruach breath of God once again just as God breathed into Adam in Genesis. He once again breathed into humanity, into the earth with His Ruach breath. He breathes on us. We breathe in the very life giving, power source of God Almighty.

Breathe and believe! How do you receive the Holy Spirit? Breathe and believe!

And they came down and prayed for them that the Samaritans might receive the Holy Spirit. Acts 8:15

If you then, evil as you are, know how to give good gifts [gifts that are to their advantage] to your children, how much more will your heavenly Father give the Holy Spirit to those who ask and continue to ask Him! Luke 11:13

The Word of God gives simple instructions in how to receive the Holy Spirit. First, you must want Him to fill your being, and move into your spirit! Next, you ask Father to give you the Holy Spirit, and Father will do just that! Finally, you must receive the gift from Father that comes from heaven and transforms your spirit with power!

The last thing you must do is yield your tongue so that the

'tongue of fire' that was given upon each of their heads in Acts chapter two becomes your forever sealing fire, changing your untamable tongue (James three) into a tongue controlled by the Holy Spirit. Now your tongue can be trusted because it is not your own. When you speak and yield to the Holy Spirit it is He who speaks through you and not your own words.

I could write so much more on how to receive the Holy Spirit, but I think you have enough Word in you now to simply trust Father to do what He says He will do. He will give you the Holy Spirit. Now you do your part and receive, then yield. That is totally up to you. Neither Father, nor Son, nor Holy Spirit will make you do anything. You are not a jiggle doll. Holy Spirit is not going to jiggle your body until a foreign language comes flowing out.

It is up to you to yield, fully and completely, yield. Yield your mind, will, and emotions. Yield your breath, tongue, and lips. Yield your belly (spirit) too. Your inner man, where your spirit resides inside you, will house the Holy Spirit for the rest of your earthly existence. He will go where you go, see what you see, hear what you allow your ears to hear. He will never leave you nor forsake you.

Receive the Holy Spirit! Speak in the language of heaven now, your spirit will be played as the instrument of the Holy Spirit!

Do not continue offering or yielding your bodily members [and faculties] to sin as instruments (tools) of wickedness. But offer and yield yourselves to God as though you have been raised from the dead to [perpetual] life, and your bodily members [and faculties] to God, presenting them as implements of righteousness. Romans 6:13

Your body, your sound, is an instrument to be played by

whomever you yield. If you yield to the devil, demons, or your own flesh then you will sound like wickedness and most certainly you have been played by the devil! If you yield to Holy Spirit, Jesus, and Father then you will be played by heaven. Whoever is playing the instrument is the sound that comes forth! Don't yield to wickedness when Holy Spirit is standing by waiting to play you with the sound of heaven.

I know when I received the Holy Spirit October 21, 1974, how much I needed a new tongue. I continue many decades later submitting my instrument, my sound, daily to His will. Will you join me?

Come into full agreement with Father that you want His gift of the Holy Spirit, and determine to receive Him. Ask Holy Spirit to fill you to overflowing with the sound from heaven. Yield your instrument fully to Him.

Speak, sing, worship, and shout in a loud and clear voice, the sound of heaven, in a new tongue that your mind does not understand.

That is how to receive the Holy Spirit.

Chapter Four
What is the Work of the Holy Spirit?

Then does He Who supplies you with His marvelous [Holy] Spirit and works powerfully and miraculously among you do so on [the ground of your doing] what the Law demands, or because of your believing in and adhering to and trusting in and relying on the message that you heard? Galatians 3:5

The work of the Holy Spirit is vast as you will see in this chapter. The first verse I want to show you is above and it says plainly that the work of the Holy Spirit is power and miracles. If those two things were the only works of the Holy Spirit that would be more than enough to know He is One of the Godhead Trinity! But there is so much more!

So too the [Holy] Spirit comes to our aid and bears us up in our weakness; for we do not know what prayer to offer nor how to offer it worthily as we ought, but the Spirit Himself goes to meet our supplication and pleads in our behalf with unspeakable yearnings and groaning too deep for utterance. Romans 8:26

The work of the Holy Spirit is to pray through us what we are incapable of praying ourselves. The Holy Spirit bears us up when we are weak. The Holy Spirit comes to our aid! When we yield ourselves and allow Holy Spirit to pray through us, then our prayers are worthy to be heard by the Righteous Judge! Holy Spirit is our Co-Counsel in the court of heaven and supplicates and pleads on our behalf legally.

While they were worshiping the Lord and fasting, the Holy Spirit said, Separate now for Me Barnabas and Saul for the work to which I have called them. Acts 13:2

The work of the Holy Spirit is multifaceted beyond our imaginations. Holy Spirit speaks to us! He calls us just as he called Barnabas and Saul for the work of the ministry.

We can see a further work of the Holy Spirit in a legal sense once again.

And He Who searches the hearts of men knows what is in the mind of the [Holy] Spirit [what His intent is], because the Spirit intercedes and pleads [before God] in behalf of the saints according to and in harmony with God's will.
Romans 8:27

Holy Spirit stands in the court of heaven before God, our Righteous Judge, and intercedes on our behalf. He pleads before the court of heaven the plea of the blood of Jesus over us! What a gift from Father to us! Oh, how He must love us to give us the Holy Spirit!

But the fruit of the [Holy] Spirit [the work which His presence within accomplishes] is love, joy (gladness), peace, patience (an even temper, forbearance), kindness, goodness, (benevolence), faithfulness, gentleness (meekness, humility), self-control (self-restraint, continence). Galatians 5:22-23a

We will further study the fruit of the Spirit in a later chapter, but notice here that the actual nine fruit of the Holy Spirit are the work of the presence of Holy Spirit within us. When we are walking in the fruit of the Holy Spirit His work within us is working! Thank You, Holy Spirit, for changing us from our old unregenerate self to this precious eternal being we become because of Your living within us!

My last scripture for the work of the Holy Spirit comes from my favorite chapter and my favorite passage from Jesus to His disciples.

And I will ask the Father, and He will give you another Comforter (Counselor, Helper, Intercessor, Advocate, Strengthener, and Standby), that He may remain with you forever - the Spirit of Truth, Whom the world cannot receive (welcome, take to its heart), because it does not see Him or know and recognize Him. But you know and recognize Him, for He lives with you [constantly] and will be in you. Jesus answered, if a person [really] loves Me, he will keep My word [obey My teaching]; and My Father will love him, and We will come to him and make Our home (abode, special dwelling place) with him. But the Comforter (Counselor, Helper, Intercessor, Advocate, Strengthener, Standby), the Holy Spirit, Whom the Father will send in My name [in My place, to represent Me and act on My behalf], He will teach you all things. And He will cause you to recall (will remind you of, bring to your remembrance) everything I have told you.
John 14:16,17, 23, 26

For me, this chapter has continually changed my life and expanded my understanding of the Holy Spirit for almost fifty years. The work of the Holy Spirit is marvelous! How could we, or why would we, ever want to live without the Holy Spirit?

*The Holy Spirit has been sent in place of Jesus.
*The Holy Spirit represents Jesus and acts on Jesus' behalf.
*The Holy Spirit will teach me all things.
*The Holy Spirit will help me to recall what I have forgotten and literally bring to my memory everything Jesus has told me through His word!
*The Holy Spirit comforts, counsels, and helps me.
*The Holy Spirit intercedes, advocates, strengthens, and is always on standby ready to help me!
*The Holy Spirit never lies to me because He is the Spirit of Truth.

What really stands out in the above verses to me is how much work the Holy Spirit does for us. Why would anyone want to reject the Holy Spirit? The verses above tell us why. When we are of the world, when we are worldly instead of heavenly minded, we CANNOT RECEIVE THE HOLY SPIRIT. Why? Jesus said if we can't see Holy Spirit, or know or recognize Holy Spirit, then we can't receive Holy Spirit.

If you have had a hard time receiving Holy Spirit in the past just take a moment of your spiritual inventory, and make sure you have not been in the position where your mind was fully in control, operating from the 'tree of knowledge' instead of receiving the 'Tree of Life'.

If you feel that has been you in the past, all is not lost! Stop right now and repent. Ask the Lord of your life, Jesus Christ, to forgive you of worldliness, to create within you a clean heart, and start fresh. Dump the world's ways including any thought life that is of this world, and ask Father God to strengthen you with the fire of His presence and purify you. This way you will be ready through purification to house the very Holy Spirit presence of God Almighty!

We will discuss the third level of baptism, the fire baptism before we are finished with this book. Many people pray the sinner's prayer, and give their lives to Jesus. Some actually make Him Lord of their lives. Even less people receive the Holy Spirit to not only be with them, but to move inside them, to be filled with His Holy Spirit, and a tiny remnant will run after His presence until the third level of fire baptism purifies them forever. I don't know about you, but I want the full work of the Holy Spirit in my life, all three levels of baptism, and all the fire from heaven that He is willing to send me, I will take!

One of the main works of the Holy Spirit in our personal lives is to guide and lead us. It takes discipline to take the time to listen to His voice. He is a still, small voice. He doesn't shout or push us to do what is right, or to go the way that is best for us. He guides us. He leads us, but He doesn't shove us!

Recently, I was trying to get direction from heaven on a particular thing, and I was praying. I was praying and praying. I was asking the Lord to tell me what to do. This went on for days and days, and in my frustration one morning in my prayer time I said to the Lord, "I wish You would speak up! I can't hear You!"

Immediately I heard Him say, "You don't want Me to shout. You would not survive My shout." It shook me to the core because I know the Spirit of the Lord, the Holy Spirit, is not moved by our frustrations and impatience. In fact, those two flesh characteristics are exactly opposite of His nature.

To be led by the Lord we must learn to listen, to obey quickly, and to be patient.

So I say to you, Ask and keep on asking and it shall be given you, seek and keep on seeking and you shall find; knock and

keep on knocking and the door shall be opened to you.
Luke 11:9

Some believe this means we have to be very demanding with our asking, but I don't believe that is what this verse is telling us at all. I believe this verse is telling us to stay consistent in our prayers. Don't be double minded, believing one day, and giving up the next. We continue to ask and keep on asking. We stay consistent and faithful. We never ever quit until the victory is ours.

Holy Spirit leads us, guides us, and directs us, but we must stay faithful whether we have a quick answer or it comes when it comes to us. Stay faithful to listen, and obey His voice.

And after the earthquake a fire, but the Lord was not in the fire; and after the fire [a sound of gentle stillness and] a still, small voice. 1 Kings 19:12

When Holy Spirit is directing us, He speaks softly to us. It is always, ultimately, our choice to obey Him. He won't pressure us, or intimidate us in any way. In fact, when God raises His voice, it quickens our mortal flesh to the point we start rising from the earth and meeting Him in the air!

For the Lord Himself will descend from heaven with a loud cry of summons, with the shout of an archangel, and with the blast of the trumpet of God. And those who have departed this life in Christ will rise first. Then we, the living ones who remain [on the earth], shall simultaneously be caught up along with [the resurrected dead] in the clouds to meet the Lord in the air; and so always (through the eternity of the eternities) we shall be with the Lord! 1Thessalonians 4:16-17

The Holy Spirit is the voice of Father to His people. We must learn to listen to His voice. We must learn to discipline our bodies to be still and hear what He is saying. We must learn to tune out the sounds of the earth, of the world's system, and quiet the sounds of others. To hear Him, He will not share your attention with everything and everyone else. Learn to be with Him to hear Him.

For the Word that God speaks is alive and full of power [making it active, operative, energizing, and effective]; it is sharper than any two-edged sword, penetrating to the dividing line of the breath of life (soul) and [the immortal] spirit, and of joints and marrow [of the deepest parts of our nature], exposing and sifting and analyzing and judging the very thoughts and purposes of the heart. Hebrews 4:12

Holy Spirit helps us separate our souls (minds, wills, emotions) from our spirits. He helps us solve all the questions like "Is this me, or the Holy Spirit?" "Is this my idea, or His idea?" "I can't tell if I came up with this in my own mind, or if He gave me this thought."

When the Word of God is speaking to us the very sound of His voice is alive! It is sharp! It divides my thoughts from His thoughts. Listen and know His voice. You will only truly know His voice after you have spent time with Him, developing the sound of His voice in your spirit.

When I was much younger and my pride was much more in the lead of my life than it is today, (I'm still working on it and will until He comes for me), I was in Hollywood and had a great agent. He continually set me up for great jobs, and one day he presented, what I thought at the time to be, the job of a lifetime.

Like always, I took everything before the Lord and presented it to Him. Most of the time I knew what He was going to say. Over the years, I had learned what to take to Him, but most things, I already knew the answer would be no. About some things I didn't even have to pray.

As you walk with the Spirit of God, the Holy Spirit, after many years, you know already what is right for your future and wrong for your future. Many times, prayer is not even necessary. Just say no, and keep moving. But this particular job seemed so perfect.

I had finished my Miss America year, and I was preaching two and three times a week. I was staying with a couple of Spirit-filled Christians very near the Los Angeles International Airport. Dr. Fred Price was my pastor, and I did my best to get back home at least once a week for service. It was usually the midweek service, and it was always a joy to be in the house of the Lord.

My agent brought this new job offer to me, and I was thrilled with the idea of it. I could still preach and travel some, and this particular offer was on nightly television which I absolutely loved. I have always felt so comfortable in front of the camera. I can just see the people in my mind when I speak to them. It was the first year for a brand-new show about to be launched called 'Entertainment Tonight.' I was offered the female host position.

I took this to the Lord, and like a little girl trying to convince her daddy that she would be safe going on a date, I talked and talked and talked when I prayed. I told Him all the wonderful scenarios that would come from this awesome opportunity and just how many more lives I could influence for the kingdom of God by taking this position.

This went on for quite a while. Finally, I stopped talking and waited for Him to speak to me. It was a while of just sitting there nervously waiting for His answer. Then He finally spoke in my heart. He said, "Before they become like you, you will become like them."

And that was it. It was over. If you truly say you love Him, you will keep His commandments. If you say you belong to Him, you will obey His voice. He had spoken. He didn't say much, but what He said still rings in my ears now even after more than forty years. "Before they become like you," that was my big argument. I will influence them for You, Father. I will affect Hollywood for Your glory.

But He knows what I can't possibly know. When He speaks to us it's always about the future. The Holy Spirit never speaks to you about your past. Never. Ever. He always speaks to you about your future. He knows. He has already been there with you in the future. Listen to Him and obey, if you want to have abundant life.

"Before they become like you, you will become like them." He was warning me that I was not as strong as I thought I was. I had just spent a year on the road traveling in the world's system as Miss America and I was still preaching and teaching and being a great light for Jesus.

He called me to do that particular job, and He graced me for it. I needed His grace for all assignments, but I could not take a job in Hollywood without His grace covering. This was the first of many jobs, and opportunities I have turned down over the last forty years, all under the instruction of the Holy Spirit, that still, small voice.

Now I look back over my life and each one of those natural opportunities would have taken me down a road of distraction, and quite possibly disaster. I thank God for the leading and guidance, the protection of the Holy Spirit. He is truly for me, not against me. He will never leave me or forsake me. Stay the course and let the work of the Holy Spirit be your daily guide.

Chapter Five
How do I Yield to the Holy Spirit?

Yielding to the Holy Spirit is a matter of my own will. It's easy to say, "I yield to You, Holy Spirit." Yes, it's so easy to say this, but very hard to do on a consistent lifestyle basis.

I am a musician, and my instrument of choice is piano. In today's world most people play a keyboard, and I most certainly can play a keyboard. But my instrument of choice is a piano! I am a trained classical pianist. I read music. I am not an illiterate musician. I know the music language; I read it, write it, and speak it. I studied to show myself approved before the Lord in this area. But none of that makes me qualified to flow on the piano in worship to the Lord. What qualifies me is my ability to yield to the Spirit of God Who wants to play me as the instrument while I play the instrument in my hands.

My instrument, whether an actual piano, a keyboard, or any other instrument, has no will. It doesn't argue with me or anyone else when being played. The instrument doesn't say, "I just don't feel like worshiping today. I don't feel worthy. I don't feel valued." The instrument doesn't say, "I feel used. Please don't play me today." No! The instrument has no will at all; it is completely able to be played by anyone.

The sounds that come forth from any instrument will sound like the one who is playing it. Of course, a piano will sound like a piano and not another instrument, but whether the sound is pleasant to hear truly depends on who is playing it.

Someone like me, who has training and decades of experience playing a piano will more likely play the instrument with pleasing sounds. But anyone can walk up to a piano and start banging away on the keys. It may not be pretty but anyone listening will know that it is the sound of a piano. Whether that piano sounds pleasant depends on who is playing it.

When you yield yourself to the Holy Spirit, you are the instrument, but He is the One playing you. You will sound like you no matter who is playing you, but whether your sound is pleasant or not, depends on who is playing you. If your flesh is playing you, you sound like flesh. If the devil, or one of his demons is playing you, you sound dark and demonic, possibly mean, hard, and angry. If the Holy Spirit is playing you, YOU SOUND LIKE HEAVEN!

Let not sin therefore rule as king in your mortal (short-lived, perishable) bodies, to make you yield to its cravings and be subject to its lusts and evil passions. Do not continue offering or yielding your bodily members [and faculties] to sin as instruments (tools) of wickedness. But offer and yield yourselves to God as though you have been raised from the dead to [perpetual] life, and your bodily members [and faculties] to God, presenting them as implements of righteousness. Romans 6:12-13

We have something pianos, guitars, and other instruments do not have. We have a will. We can choose to be played and by whom. A natural instrument is played by whomever touches it whether good or bad. We get to choose. We are the instrument (even when we are playing a natural instrument). We are the instrument being played by either wickedness or righteousness. How do you yield to the Holy Spirit? You practice.

To become a great musician, one must spend their lives practicing. If you don't practice, no matter how gifted you are, or talented you are, you don't improve if you don't practice. Practice, practice, practice . . . a lifetime of practice is what makes you and keeps you yielded to the Holy Spirit.

How do I yield to the Holy Spirit? You start by saying it, by confessing it, by praying it. Father, I yield myself to Your Spirit. I yield my body, my instrument to You, to be played by You. Then after you have made your decision, you do it. You stop playing yourself, and you let Him play you.

It will take a lifetime of practice to become yielded continually, and you will have to stay yielded to His Spirit, which means a prayer life that keeps you in constant communication and communion with the Holy Spirit. If you don't consciously and purposely spend time with the Holy Spirit, you can never learn to listen, hear, and obey His voice.

Stay in the secret place with Him regularly, constantly. Don't allow the Holy Spirit to visit within you; let Him move in and live, dwell within your being for eternity. It's an act of your will to allow Him access to the controls of your life.

Then there came a voice out of the cloud, saying, This is My Son, My Chosen One or My Beloved; listen to and yield to and obey Him! Luke 9:35

Father gave specific instructions from the Shekinah cloud that covered the three disciples (Peter, John, and James) along with Jesus that day. He spoke directly to them from the voice of the Holy Spirit through the cloud. He said, "Yield, listen, and obey Jesus!" Then Jesus told them the Holy Spirit would come and represent Him after the ascension, and they were to continue to listen, yield, and obey His voice.

How can we yield to a voice we don't recognize? How can we recognize a voice we don't know? We must get to know the Holy Spirit, and become intimately acquainted with Him to be able to trust Him enough to listen, yield, and obey His voice.

Spend your lifetime learning Who the Holy Spirit is to you personally. This is not head knowledge, or something you can learn from reading or a teaching that I am writing. I am talking about getting alone with Holy Spirit, every day, all day, learning how to be with Him. He will never leave you or forsake you, but you must learn how to never leave Him or forsake Him. That is the real and true challenge of your life.

Once you stop leaving Him and forsaking Him, then and only then, can you learn how to listen, yield, and obey Him, through your divine intimate covenant connection. This is how we become His bride. We stop resisting His Spirit that is trying to make us ready for His return. The Holy Spirit is trying to prepare the bride within you for His coming. The bridegroom is coming, go out to meet Him! But are you ready? Are you so intimately connected to His Spirit that you know His voice, and He knows you?

It's not enough that you know Him; He must know you. Matthew chapter twenty-five is one of my favorite parables in the Bible that Jesus taught. It is about the ten virgins who were ready and waiting for the return of the bridegroom.

They were ready and waiting. But the bridegroom tarried and didn't come as soon as they thought he would come. While they waited, half of them got 'less and less' ready. By the time the shout came, the call came forth in verse six at midnight, *Behold, the bridegroom! Go out to meet him!*

Then all ten virgins got up and put their own lamps in order. Their lamps represent the light within them. How much light do you have on reserve while you wait for the coming of the Lord? What makes the light within us continue to shine?

Verse eight gives us the answer to that question. *And the foolish said to the wise, Give us some of your oil, for our lamps are going out.*

The oil is the Holy Spirit in our lives. You may have received Jesus as Savior, but unless He was given lordship over your life, unless you went to the next level and received the Holy Spirit within your spirit, you may not have enough oil to last the waiting period of time that is happening right now! We are in a holding pattern waiting for King Jesus to come and get His bride!

Holy Spirit cannot be borrowed from someone else. You can't have enough Holy Spirit by hanging with people who have enough Holy Spirit. You must have your own reserves of oil. You must have your own supply of oil that never runs out!

But the wise replied, There will not be enough for us and for you, go instead to the dealers and buy for yourselves. But while they were going away to buy, the bridegroom came, and those who were prepared went in with him to the marriage feast; and the door was shut. Later the other virgins also came and said, Lord, Lord, open [the door] to us! But He replied, I solemnly declare to you, I do not know you [I am not acquainted with you]. Watch therefore [give strict attention and be cautious and active], for you know neither the day nor the hour when the Son of Man will come. Matthew 25:9-13

The oil that you have cannot be shared with someone who has less oil. My walk (yield) with Holy Spirit is personal. Your walk (yield) with Holy Spirit is personal. It is completely your choice whether you stay in constant fellowship with Holy Spirit filling yourself up, and even storing reserve oil, for times ahead that we know not of.

What is being freely given now will cost you when it is too late. Those without enough oil had to go and purchase, to buy more oil. And while they were doing that, He came and it was too late for them. You cannot put off for tomorrow what Holy Spirit is prompting you to do today. Delayed obedience is disobedience no matter how you want to dress it up.

When you put off until it is convenient for you what the Holy Spirit is telling you to do, you are walking out of the will of Father and from Matthew twenty-five, we can easily see that this is a very dangerous position to find yourself. Don't delay to obey. Listen, yield, obey, as Father told Peter, James, and John.

How do I keep the oil flowing? Well, we have a wonderful story to teach us how to do that.

Now the wife of a son of the prophets cried to Elisha, Your servant my husband is dead, and you know that your servant feared the Lord. But the creditor has come to take my two sons to be his slaves. Elisha said to her, What shall I do for you? Tell me, what have you [of sale value] in the house? She said, Your handmaid has nothing in the house except a jar of oil. Then he said, Go around and borrow vessels from all your neighbors, empty vessels-and not a few. And when you come in, shut the door upon you and your sons. Then pour out [the oil you have] *into all those vessels, setting aside each one when it is full. So she went from him and shut the door upon herself and her sons, who brought to her the vessels as she poured the oil. When the vessels were all full, she said to her son, Bring me another vessel. And he said to her, There is not a one left. Then the oil stopped multiplying.* 2 Kings 4:1-6

Both passages of scripture have some common principles. Matthew spoke of 'shutting the door' and the prophet told the wife and mother to shut the door. These represent timelines. These show us there are times and seasons for obeying the Holy Spirit, and then the door closes and it's over. There is no going back and deciding to obey once the door is shut. Please do not put off what the Holy Spirit is telling you to do. Don't wait until the door is shut, and you have no more opportunity to yield and obey His voice.

Also notice the prophet told her to go and borrow vessels to pour what little bit of oil she had. He did not tell her to go borrow oil. Why? Because no one else's oil will work for you. She could only use the oil she had. Do you have enough oil?

It was not about how much oil she had but what oil she had! Her husband was a prophet, and she had a little jar of oil, his anointing oil, that he used for ministry. This was not a jar of cooking oil; this was the holy oil of her husband, the prophet. It was not about the quantity of oil in this case. It was about the quality of anointing on the oil and her obedience to yield and obey the voice of the prophet.

How do you keep the oil flowing in your own personal life? Pour! The more you pour the oil, the oil will continue to multiply. The moment you have no one else (no vessel to pour into) the oil will stop. Beloved, keep pouring your oil wherever you find a vessel that will receive it! The more you pour, the more oil you will have! He will never leave you. The oil will never stop multiplying unless you decide you are done and quit pouring.

None of us will ever have enough money to buy enough oil of the Holy Spirit. The anointing of God, the Holy Spirit is not for sale. The only thing we have of enough value to receive more of the oil of Holy Spirit is to yield our bodies and souls completely to His control. Our yield, our obedience, our desire to listen and obey causes a flow of the Holy Spirit within us that cannot be tapped or controlled by humanity.

Chapter Six
What are the Gifts of the Holy Spirit?

Now about the spiritual gifts (the special endowments of supernatural energy), brethren, I do not want you to be misinformed. You know that when you were heathen, you were led off after idols that could not speak [habitually] as impulse directed and whenever the occasion might arise. Therefore, I want you to understand that no one speaking under the power and influence of the [Holy] Spirit of God can [ever] say, Jesus be cursed! And no one can [really] say, Jesus is [my] Lord, except by and under the power and influence of the Holy Spirit. Now there are distinctive varieties and distributions of endowments (gifts, extraordinary powers distinguishing certain Christians, due to the power of divine grace operating in their souls by the Holy Spirit) and they vary, but the [Holy] Spirit remains the same. And there are distinctive varieties of service and ministration, but it is the same Lord [Who is served]. And there are distinctive varieties of operation [of working to accomplish things], but it is the same God Who inspires and energizes them all in all. But to each one is given the manifestation of the [Holy] Spirit [the evidence, the

spiritual illumination of the Spirit] for good and profit. To one is given in and through the [Holy] Spirit [the power to speak] a message of wisdom, and to another [the power to express] a word of knowledge and understanding according to the same [Holy] Spirit; to another [wonder-working] faith by the same [Holy] Spirit, to another the extraordinary powers of healing by the one Spirit; to another the working of miracles, to another prophetic insight (the gift of interpreting the divine will and purpose); to another the ability to discern and distinguish between [the utterances of true] spirits [and false ones], to another various kinds of [unknown] tongues, to another the ability to interpret [such] tongues. All these [gifts, achievements, abilities] are inspired and brought to pass by one and the same [Holy] Spirit, Who apportions to each person individually [exactly] as He chooses.
1 Corinthians 12:1-11

We will read further in a moment, but I want you to see how perfectly and clearly the scripture is about the gifts of the Holy Spirit. There are several numbers that represent the Holy Spirit, and the number nine is one of them. We will discuss in a later chapter why this particular number is the Holy Spirit's heavenly number.

The number fifty is also a number that represents the Holy Spirit. This number represents the expression of the Holy Spirit on the earth and His relationship with mankind as He was given to mankind on the 50th day after Jesus Christ's resurrection. Holy Spirit was given ten days after Christ's ascension, but the number nine is the most specific number for the manifestation of the Holy Spirit.

As we study in the chapter on the Hierarchy of the Kingdom of God you will see the full dimension of the vertical expression of why this number nine touches humanity in a special and divinely eternal way. But for now, let's look at the obvious reasons why number nine is the expressed manifestation of the Holy Spirit.

In 1 Corinthians chapter twelve we see the list of nine manifestations of the gifts of the Holy Spirit. I began in the scripture passage with the first few verses because I wanted you to notice the Bible calls these nine gifts, spiritual gifts, special endowments of supernatural energy. That is pretty cool! Paul went on to say that he did not want the people to be misinformed.

In all my fifty years of walking with Holy Spirit I would easily say the most misinformed topic in the body of Christ must be the Holy Spirit. The devil and demons work overtime to make sure people are afraid of the Holy Spirit's gifts and confused about these gifts. The devil and his cohorts try and spread rumors and lies in this area and bring chaos to the minds of people, so they won't receive the Holy Spirit and the gifts that come with Him into their lives.

When I have taught on the Holy Spirit's gifts, and when I have heard others speak on this subject, I have never noticed verse two and what Paul was saying to the people. He told them that their heathen idol gods could not speak habitually as impulse directed and whenever the occasion might arise. I have never noticed this verse before. He was telling them that the Holy Spirit is the opposite of their heathen dead gods. The Holy Spirit can speak habitually as impulse directed and whenever the occasion might arise!

The Holy Spirit habitually speaks through us! He doesn't always send us a plan that on Thursday night at 8:00PM I will be speaking through you! Nope! That is not how the Holy Spirit moves. He is habitually wanting to move through you, speaking through you. It would seem, almost impulsively, He would want to speak through you whenever there is a need or occasion where the Holy Spirit has something to say!

Then Paul went on in verse three to say that he wanted the people to understand that when a person is speaking under the power and influence of the Holy Spirit that those same people can't curse the name of Jesus or say that Jesus is cursed. He also qualified to them that when a person is not controlled by the Holy Spirit that they cannot say that Jesus is my Lord. This statement is made under the influence of and by the power of the Holy Spirit speaking through us!

These are very easily seen qualifying statements that help us when discerning whether a person is actually speaking under the control of the Holy Spirit, or their own spirit is in control of their mouths. What does this mean to us? When we are listening to a message, or reading someone's book, notice, listen, and hear what they are saying. Use the power of the Holy Spirit's gifts that are already within you to discern the words of another person.

Out of the abundance of the heart the mouth speaks. No one speaks for long under their own power that their mouth does not give way to flesh instead of pretending to be Holy Spirit controlled. We must listen to know what is in another person's spirit.

The gifts of the Holy Spirit are beyond our natural abilities, beyond our natural intellect, and beyond our creativity and personal power. The gifts of the Holy Spirit come with the package of the Holy Spirit. There are nine manifestations of the gifts of the Holy Spirit. According to the verses we just read these gifts are given for the good and profit of others. They are not to elevate the one who is being used, or cause any pride or self-adulation. The Holy Spirit gifts are given through humanity to help others.

But to each one is given the manifestation of the Holy Spirit which is the evidence, and the spiritual illumination of the Spirit for good and profit. 1 Corinthians 12:7

Without the manifestation of the Holy Spirit through His gifts there is no evidence of Holy Spirit living inside you. This would be like going to court and pleading your case of innocence and having no evidence to prove your innocence. When Holy Spirit lives inside you there will be evidence of His existence operating through you at all times, whenever the occasion arises for the need of that evidence.

When Holy Spirit can help a person through His gifts flowing through you, He will want to break through your mind, will, and emotions and your flesh body, too. He will want to escape the prison you have built around Him with your soul and body. He wants to manifest! He wants others to experience His presence and power through you!

Don't ask Holy Spirit to come and live inside you just to house Him in the prison of your unresolved soul and flesh issues. Come on! Get over yourself, and allow Holy Spirit to come forth.

When a person asks Holy Spirit to come and live in them, not just with them, but in them, as Jesus spoke of in John chapter fourteen, at that moment your own spirit has been given the greatest level of power available to humanity. If you choose to not allow your spirit to be under the control of the Holy Spirit, then you will struggle and wrestle between your power filled spirit and your self-fed, self-controlled soul and flesh.

You ask Holy Spirit to fill you to overflowing, then you shut Him down because your soul and / or flesh still want to be in the lead. No wonder people struggle with allowing the river of living water to come bursting forth from their spirit being when the hard shell of their flesh, or the scared unbroken realm of their soul, still controls their very lives, which in turn, controls their mouths.

People ask to be filled with the Holy Spirit, but try and use an unbridled tongue to speak the things of heaven. That is why when the Holy Spirit was first given in Acts chapter two the room was filled with the 'sound of heaven' and there appeared 'tongues of fire' that sat upon each one of their heads. Until we stop trying to speak in tongues using our flesh untamable tongue (according to James chapter three) and receive our tongue of fire on our heads, and yield to that heavenly tongue, our ability to speak in tongues will never be pure and holy. At best we will work hard at it, and try, try, and try again . . . which is nothing more than human works and is unfruitful.

I want to learn to yield here on earth so that when I enter heaven, I have already attained a higher level of living and being. I want to enter heaven already knowing my heavenly language!

I have multi-dimensional expressions and manifestations of who I am that have developed over my lifetime. I was born a girl, a daughter to my parents, and a sister to my siblings. I grew up and became a friend to many. I studied and learned and developed my manifested expression of being a student, and a musician.

Eventually I became Miss America, and later on met and married Harry Salem. So that brought about a new manifested expression of who I am, a wife, then three born children later, I became a mother to Harry, Roman, and Gabrielle. As life progressed Roman married Stephanie. Roman and Stephanie gave birth to two beautiful grandchildren for us, Mia Gabrielle, and Roman Harry. Now I am Emma. This could be my most favorite manifested expression of who I am!

During these same years I was developing into a preacher, teacher, and even healer, just like my Jesus! I would now describe myself as a worshiper, and that is most certainly one of His manifested expressions through me.

Why am I telling you all this, and how does it relate to the Holy Spirit's gifts? I am a human being, and even I have many expressions that manifest who I am, depending on who I am with, and what occasion is arising at that moment. When I am with my little mama in MS, I am still her daughter. When I am with Mia and Little Romey, I am most definitely Emma! Whatever occasion may arise at any given moment in time who you are will burst forth in manifestation expressed through you!

When you receive the Holy Spirit into your spirit, He has nine manifested expressions through His nine gifts. He wants to manifest those gifts through you at any given moment that the occasion should arise.

1. Word of wisdom
2. Word of knowledge
3. Gift of faith
4. Gift of healings
5. Working of miracles
6. Gift of prophesy
7. Discerning of spirits
8. Different kinds of tongues
9. Interpretation of tongues

These nine gifts are all from the same Holy Spirit who will move from being with you to being in you. He will be housed inside your spirit, who is inside your soul, that is inside your flesh body. He moves into a human being so He can express Himself through His persona of manifested gifts.

You are the instrument. The Holy Spirit wants to play you. The first and easiest gift to show evidence of the infilling of the Holy Spirit is the eighth gift, different kinds of tongues. Notice in Acts chapter two when they were all filled with the Holy Spirit that immediately they all began to speak in different languages, different tongues as the Spirit gave them utterance.

Now there were then residing in Jerusalem Jews, devout and God-fearing men from every country under heaven. And when this sound was heard, this multitude came together and they were astonished and bewildered, because each one heard them [the apostles] speaking in his own [particular] dialect. And they were beside themselves with amazement, saying, Are not all these who are talking Galileans? Then how is it that we hear, each of us, in our own (particular) dialect to which we were born? Acts 2:5-8

It was that gift in manifestation that caused all the people to notice this humble united group of one hundred and twenty people. Once the other people all heard them speaking in tongues they gathered around and then could feel the power coming from them. No one was afraid anymore.

The power of the Holy Spirit eradicated all fear from the group! It wasn't very long that over three thousand people gave their hearts to Jesus! The power of the Holy Spirit activated in your life isn't for you! It is for the good and profit of others. The Holy Spirit's power inside you causes others to want what you have! The Holy Spirit wants to touch humanity, but He needs your instrument, your vessel, to house Him. People meet the Holy Spirit through the Holy Spirit dwelling in you!

Peter was so filled with the Holy Spirit that power came upon him to preach, and preach he did! He preached a powerful message of Jesus Christ to that massive group of Jewish people. They responded with conviction in their hearts in questions of what must we do?

Repent (change your views and purpose to accept the will of God in your inner selves instead of rejecting it) and be baptized, every one of you, in the name of Jesus Christ for the forgiveness of and release from your sins; and you shall receive the gift of the Holy Spirit. For the promise [of the Holy Spirit] is to and for you and your children, and to and for all that are far away, [even] to and for as many as the Lord our God invites and bids to come to Himself. And [Peter] solemnly and earnestly witnessed (testified) and admonished (exhorted) with much more continuous speaking and warned (reproved, advised, and encouraged) them, saying, Be saved from this crooked (perverse, wicked, unjust) generation. Therefore, those who accepted and welcomed his message were baptized, and there were added that day about 3,000 souls.
Acts 2:38-41

Because of Peter being filled with the Holy Spirit, he had the power of the Holy Spirit flowing through him. He was not afraid to boldly preach Jesus to those who were making fun, and mocking those who were speaking in tongues. This same man who denied his even knowing Jesus right before His crucifixion was now in the midst of the same people, and under the power that was living inside of his spirit, Peter was leading them to Jesus!

But the person who is united to the Lord becomes one spirit with Him. 1 Corinthians 6:17

Once Peter allowed the Holy Spirit to move inside his spirit, and he yielded his tongue, body, mind, and soul to Holy Spirit he became one with the Lord. Once you truly become one, united to the Lord through the power of the Holy Spirit, you shall receive power!

But you shall receive power (ability, efficiency, and might) when the Holy Spirit has come upon you, and you shall be My witnesses in Jerusalem and all Judea and Samaria and to the end (the very bounds) of the earth. Acts 1:8

Peter received the Holy Spirit, and with Him came His power, His might, His ability, His efficiency, and all His nine gifts! All of Holy Spirit is available to us and through us when we finally yield our entire triune being to Him.

Holy Spirit wants to flow through you to help others, to benefit others, to manifest Who He is to others! I am not saying that you won't personally benefit from housing the very Spirit of God! You will benefit! You will become one, unified, with the Lord through Holy Spirit. But the gifts of the Holy Spirit are given to flow through you to help others. Those nine gifts are always inside of you as long as Holy Spirit is inside of you. And He has already promised that He will never leave you or forsake you.

The gifts of the Holy Spirit don't wane or burn out, but people do, when they try to operate the gifts in their own strength and ability. The gifts of the Holy Spirit flowing through you energize you, and charge you with power like you have never known, supernatural extraordinary power that distinguishes you from other people!

Holy Spirit does not need you to try. In fact, it's the exact opposite. Holy Spirit needs you to get out of the way, mentally, emotionally, religiously, and physically. I can hear Him saying inside of me right now, "Get out of the way please. I don't need your help! I need your yield."

Holy Spirit always remains the same. He is supernatural. He

is not a circus act. Many people are so enthralled with the spectacular that they totally miss the supernatural move of Holy Spirit. He does not give His gifts in operation to entertain people. He is not in the entertainment business, in fact, quite the opposite. The moment the attention of people is focused on the gifts and not on the Lord, the gifts seem to cease to flow. The moment we stop pouring out, but start manufacturing the 'pour,' the oil dries up.

These gifts are amazing and for us, but must not become what we seek. The moment people think that speaking in tongues is what they are receiving they seem to receive nothing from that point on until they 'fix their thinking.' We are receiving the Holy Spirit, the very Spirit of our Father God.

We are receiving one of the Godhead to live inside our spirits. The gift of tongues is simply one of nine manifested gifts of Who moved into our very beings! All gifts are available as He sees the need for any one or all of them to flow!

So there is one Holy Spirit given by Father because Jesus, the Son of God, asked His Father, Who is now our Father through Jesus Christ to send to us, the Holy Spirit. The Holy Spirit came to be the representative of Jesus Christ to us as humanity who would receive Jesus as our Lord. Then we must receive Holy Spirit to live inside our human spirits. Our human spirit becomes one with Holy Spirit, and we house Him.

Do you not know that your body is the temple (the very sanctuary) of the Holy Spirit Who lives with you, Whom you have received [as a Gift] from God? 1 Corinthians 6:19

You are the temple, the very sanctuary of the living God. You take Holy Spirit everywhere you go. When you speak (yielded to Holy Spirit) Holy Spirit speaks through you. You introduce everyone you come in contact with to Holy Spirit. Whether you ever say the words or not, you are constantly introducing Holy Spirit to humanity. "Holy Spirit, may I introduce you to my neighbor, so and so. Neighbor so and so, let me introduce you to Holy Spirit."

If you try to represent Holy Spirit then all is lost. He does not need us to represent Him. He needs us to introduce Him. If you try to represent Holy Spirit you will become burned out, exhausted, and want to quit. But when you simply yield, and get out of the way, Holy Spirit will do the work of the ministry, and you get to come along for the ride!

Pray this prayer with me.

Holy Spirit, I ask You to work through me. Teach me to get out and stay out of Your way through my outer shell of a body, and my inner shell of a soul. Teach me how to stay broken without having to be broken over and over again.

Come to the forefront of my triune being and never retreat. Forgive me when I try to force You back inside, when I need You more than ever to lead me daily! In Jesus' mighty name, I yield myself to You, Amen.

Chapter Seven
What is the Fruit of the Holy Spirit?

But I say, walk and live [habitually] in the [Holy] Spirit [responsive to and controlled and guided by the Spirit]; then you will certainly not gratify the cravings and desires of the flesh (of human nature without God). For the desires of the flesh are opposed to the [Holy] Spirit, and the [desires of the] Spirit are opposed to the flesh (godless human nature); for these are antagonistic to each other [continually withstanding and in conflict with each other], so that you are not free but are prevented from doing what you desire to do. But if you are guided (led) by the [Holy] Spirit, you are not subject to the Law. Now the doings (practices) of the flesh are clear (obvious): they are immorality, impurity, indecency, idolatry, sorcery, enmity, strife, jealousy, anger (ill temper), selfishness, divisions (dissensions), party spirit (factions, sects with peculiar opinions, heresies), envy, drunkenness, carousing, and the like. I warn you beforehand, just as I did previously, that those who do such things shall not inherit the kingdom of God. But the fruit of the [Holy] Spirit [the work which His presence within accomplishes] is love, joy (gladness), peace, patience (an even temper, forbearance), kindness, goodness (benevolence), faithfulness, gentleness (meekness, humility), self-control (self-restraint, continence). Against such things there is no law [that can bring a charge]. And those who belong to Christ Jesus (the Messiah) have crucified the flesh (the godless human nature) with its passions and appetites and desires. If we live by the [Holy] Spirit, let us also walk by the Spirit. [If by the Holy Spirit we have our life in God, let us go forward walking in line, our conduct controlled by the Spirit.] Let us not become vainglorious and self-conceited, competitive and challenging and provoking and irritating to one another, envying and being jealous of one another. Galatians 5:16-26

I realize this is quite a long passage of scripture, but I want you to see this in context and not just pull out the nine fruit of the Holy Spirit. The first thing I want you to notice is in the previous chapter when we were discussing the 'gifts' of the Holy Spirit, that gifts are plural. There are nine distinct and different gifts all given to us through the infilling of the Holy Spirit. When Holy Spirit moves inside of our spirit and we house the Spirit of God, from that point on we have all the gifts that are manifestations of His persona. His gifts flow through us to others, for the good and profit of others.

When we read this passage of scripture concerning the fruit of the Holy Spirit the very first thing I notice is fruit is not plural, but rather is singular fruit. This is easiest to visualize when you think of the sections of an orange. The orange is one fruit but there are many sections within it. One fruit, many sections, easily show us how the fruit of the Spirit manifests different levels of walking in the Holy Spirit.

In the Galatians passage of scripture, the first 'list' you see is not the fruit of the Holy Spirit but rather the 'doings, practices' of the flesh. The Bible states that this list is very clear and obvious. Most Christians dismiss their list of ongoing flesh practices as if it is not a big deal. But the scripture lists the practices of the flesh and make known the outcome of such practices. Let's look at this list first.

1. Immorality
2. Impurity
3. Indecency
4. Idolatry
5. Sorcery
6. Enmity
7. Strife
8. Jealousy
9. Anger, ill temper
10. Selfishness
11. Divisions, dissensions
12. Party spirit - factions, sects with peculiar opinions, heresies
13. Envy
14. Drunkenness
15. Carousing
16. And the like . . .

These flesh practices disqualify us from inheriting the kingdom of God. The Bible states that practicing flesh works will cause you to lose your inheritance in the kingdom of God.

I don't know about you but I have to repent before I can go on with my writing. I fall into the trap of doing one or two, sometimes more, of these flesh works almost every day. I can get frustrated and instead of stopping and praying in the Holy Spirit, which would begin to produce the fruit of the Spirit, I instead, give in to the frustration and begin to practice works of the flesh.

I can get angry at things, situations, and even people. I can easily get into an ill temper over the simplest of things. Even though I don't think I would ever fall trap to drunkenness since I don't drink alcohol or even consider 'carousing' around, selfishness, self-pity, jealousy, strife, and envying others are a regular flesh practice I have to repent of. I am not in any way excusing these actions. I am repenting of them, turning my back on them, and asking Holy Spirit to put His fire on my head to help burn them out of my thinking, and way of being.

I have stopped and asked Father to forgive me of these traps of the enemy through my own flesh. It seems almost every trap I fall into starts with self-focus, selfishness. Yes, selfishness is listed in the practices. Selfishness is a work of the flesh.

But understand this, that in the last days will come (set in) perilous times of great stress and trouble [hard to deal with and hard to bear]. For people will be lovers of self and [utterly] self-centered, lovers of money and aroused by an inordinate [greedy] desire for wealth, proud and arrogant and contemptuous boasters. They will be abusive (blasphemous, scoffing), disobedient to parents, ungrateful, unholy and profane. [They will be] without natural [human] affection (callous and inhuman), relentless (admitting of no truce or appeasement); [they will be] slanderers (false accusers, troublemakers), intemperate and loose in morals and conduct, uncontrolled and fierce, haters of good. [They will be] treacherous [betrayers], rash, [and] inflated with self-conceit. [They will be] lovers of sensual pleasures and vain amusements more than and rather than lovers of God. For [although] they hold a form of piety (true religion), they deny and reject and are strangers to the power of it [their conduct belies the genuineness of their profession]. Avoid [all] such people [turn away from them]. For among them are those who worm their way into homes and captivate silly and weak-natured and spiritually dwarfed women, loaded down with

[the burden of their] sins [and easily] swayed and led away by various evil desires and seductive impulses. [These weak women will listen to anybody, who will teach them]; they are forever inquiring and getting information, but are never able to arrive at a recognition and knowledge of the Truth. Now just as Jannes and Jambres were hostile to and resisted Moses, so these men also are hostile to and oppose the Truth. They have depraved and distorted minds, and are reprobate and counterfeit and to be rejected as far as the faith is concerned. But they will not get very far, for their rash folly will become obvious to everybody, as was that of those [magicians mentioned]. Now you have closely observed and diligently followed my teaching, conduct, purpose in life, faith, patience, love, steadfastness, persecutions, sufferings - such as occurred to me at Antioch, at Iconium, and at Lystra, persecutions I endured, but out of them all the Lord delivered me.
2 Timothy 3:1-11

It is hard for me to stop writing the scripture in this particular chapter because it ties so perfectly with the 'cancel' culture of today. We must not fall trap to flesh practices simply because they become the normal culture of today. Flesh is still flesh and as the Galatians passage told us, it is in opposition to the Holy Spirit within us. When you fall trap to flesh works, stop and repent immediately as I shared above. Don't wait; don't dismiss it as just flesh. Flesh is opposed to the Holy Spirit. It is not a little thing to be dismissed but rather an immediate response of repentance must come forth from us!

In that list of flesh actions, works, and practices I hope you noticed how many of them were rooted in 'self.' If we can only overcome our own self focus, in a culture that promotes taking care of me, we have won a great majority of the battles over 'flesh.'

I spent a little time on the opposite of the fruit of the Spirit so it will be easier to notice that every fruit of the Holy Spirit is focused outward toward humanity and not inward toward me. Even though I greatly benefit when I walk in the fruit of the Holy Spirit, so too, does everyone who has to be around me. Let's look at the sections of the fruit in the order that Galatians chapter five lists them.

1. Love
2. Joy (gladness)
3. Peace
4. Patience (an even temper, forbearance)
5. Kindness
6. Goodness (benevolence)
7. Faithfulness
8. Gentleness (meekness, humility)
9. Self-control (self-restraint, continence)

In Galatians chapter five verse twenty-two we see how we can walk in the fruit of the Spirit. The verse states that the fruit of the Holy Spirit, the work which His presence within accomplishes, is exactly how we become fruitful. We can never 'fruit' the Holy Spirit until His presence is within us and controls us. Once He has moved inside our spirits, and our bodies house His presence, then and only then, can we begin to produce the fruit of the Holy Spirit.

Without the Holy Spirit living within us we are hopeless to produce anything other than our flesh practices. With the Holy Spirit inside of our spirits, we can begin 'fruiting' His presence rather than our own.

As I have studied this for many years, I truly believe the fruit of the Holy Spirit is given in an order that we actually produce first, love. Then once we have accomplished that fruit of the Holy Spirit, then the section of the fruit, joy comes forth. When we begin to fruit the very first section of Holy Spirit fruit, we are more able to love people who aren't necessarily walking where we walk. We are able to get along with people who don't always agree with us. Why? Because we are fruiting the first section of the Holy Spirit's fruit.

The Holy Spirit's love allows us to cover the sins of others instead of walking in judgment that always wants to expose their sins. A good way to check your first section of fruit is how you talk about others. Are you always covering them from the judgments of others or are you 'throwing them into the lion's den' by exposing and gossiping about them? And don't think the Holy Spirit doesn't notice when you try to disguise your judgment as an intercessor, or prayer warrior for them.

You spread your gossip under the disguise of asking another to join you in prayer, and yet no prayer is ever uttered, just gossiping judgment. One must check their own motives and sheriff their own lives. The Holy Spirit will help us do this if we will only listen. *Love covers a multitude of sins.* 1 Peter 4:8

The second section of Holy Spirit's fruit is joy. Once you are truly fruiting love from your very being, then the next section of Holy Spirit fruit will begin to emerge. Joy! *The joy of the Lord is our strength.* Nehemiah 8:10

Your strength will return to you. You will no longer be exhausted and worn out all the time. You will stop talking about quitting, and being burned out, and you can begin to 'run and not be weary; walk and not faint.'

The third section of Holy Spirit fruit is peace. *The peace that passes all understanding, intellect, or soul realm, will begin to keep your hearts and minds in Christ Jesus.* Philippians 4:7

I truly believe the fruit of the Holy Spirit comes out through us in levels. Once we begin to understand how to fruit love, then we are filled with unexplainable joy, that produces a peace that is not logical or rational, but rather overrides our natural abilities to understand.

This kind of peace survives circumstances, and situations, and what's going on around us. This kind of foundation built upon the fruit of the Holy Spirit cannot be shaken no matter what comes our way. Natural disasters, or demonic storms can't shake the foundation of love, joy, and peace fruiting from the presence of the Holy Spirit living within us.

Patience is the fourth level of Holy Spirit fruit and this is the one section of Holy Spirit that I seem to have to learn over and over again. I believe that until we master love, joy, and peace, no patience fruit can ever be consistent in our lives. This is not to say that we won't have moments of patience, but the fruit of the Holy Spirit is not about having moments of each section of fruitfulness.

When Holy Spirit is truly fruiting in our lives it is when others can't be patient that we are the most patient. His fruitfulness goes against our natural personalities. His fruitfulness goes against who we naturally are! This is not about being natural anymore. This is about becoming a supernatural person, walking, living, and breathing in a natural world.

If one is naturally patient then it is not the fruit of the Holy Spirit, but rather your own personality that is shown. The fruit of the Holy Spirit is in opposition to your naturalness.

I am more naturally patient with people around me when I am well rested. That is not the fruit of the Holy Spirit. The fruit of the Holy Spirit is when I am exhausted and my body is very tired. My patience is totally being tried by people, circumstances, and situations around me, and I fruit patience. That's when I know it is the Holy Spirit's patient fruitfulness manifesting in my life.

I believe Holy Spirit builds a foundation within us for a true temple for God's presence. Remember our bodies are the temple of the Holy Spirit. He moves into our beings and begins to build His temple within us! These very foundations keep us when the storms are raging, the rains are falling, and the mud slides of life begin to try and overtake us. What kind of foundation is built within you? The rains are going to come. The quakes are going to quake. Everything that can be shaken will be shaken!

He has given us nine levels of foundations that we can allow Holy Spirit to build within our temples. The first foundation is love. Until we have that first foundation built within us we cannot build the second foundation level of joy, then the third of peace, the fourth of patience, the fifth level of kindness, the sixth level of goodness, seventh level of faithfulness, eighth level of gentleness, and the final foundational level in our lives of self-control.

When we realize this is not a list that we can 'pick and choose' from, but rather we build our temple foundations based upon these levels of fruitfulness, we can begin to see then how each one builds upon the other. With the final level of self-control only manifesting in our lives after we have mastered the first eight fruits it begins to make more sense to us why each fruit (level) is so very important. Like all things I have learned as I have walked with God, we are on a journey within us, and there are no shortcuts, only specific ways through to victory. So many people want to have the ninth level manifesting in their lives of self-control when they have not yet mastered walking in love! Love is the first and most foundational level in our walk with God.

1 John chapter three lines out verse by verse when we are filled with Holy Spirit then we won't practice sin, but rather we will practice loving one another. There are no other options for truly knowing and manifesting God other than when we love one another and walk in this love no matter what is happening in our lives.

For this is the message (the announcement) which you have heard from the first, that we should love one another. 1 John 3:11

We know that we have passed over out of death into Life by the fact that we love the brethren (our fellow Christians). He who does not love abides (remains, is held and kept continually) in [spiritual] death. 1 John 3:14

Then the final verses in that chapter seal the revelation and the correlation between truly being saved and walking in love.

Little children, let us not love [merely] in theory or in speech but in deed and in truth (in practice and in sincerity). By this we shall come to know (perceive, recognize, and understand) that we are of the Truth, and can reassure (quiet, conciliate, and pacify) our hearts in His presence . . . And this is His order (His command, His injunction): that we should believe in (put our faith and trust in and adhere to and rely on) the name of His Son Jesus Christ (the Messiah), and that we should love one another, just as He has commanded us. All who keep His commandments [who obey His orders and follow His plan, live and continue to live, to stay and] abide in Him, and He in them. [They let Christ be a home to them and they are the home of Christ.] And by this we know and understand and have the proof that He [really] lives and makes His home in us: by the [Holy] Spirit Whom He has given us.
1 John 3:18-19, 23-24

There can be no clearer verses than these to tell us when we are filled with the Holy Spirit we will be filled with His fruitfulness. His foundational levels of the Holy Spirit's fruitfulness in us is how everyone knows that our spirits have united and become one with the Holy Spirit. If you say you are filled with the Holy Spirit but don't manifest the very first level as evidence of that, then it is easy for all to discern that you are not telling the truth.

The truth is when the Spirit of Truth fills your spirit, wall to wall, floor to ceiling, so to speak, then love is your first response to trouble. Joy is your second response, peace your third response, patience your fourth response, kindness, goodness, faithfulness, gentleness and finally self-control. You have built your Holy Spirit foundation within your temple that carries you through anything that tries to come your way.

The way you respond to circumstances, situations and trouble tell all observing you, who or what you are full of. I have said this for many years, you will always manifest what you are full of. If you are filled to overflowing with the Holy Spirit, He will always be what you manifest!

Let's look back at the remaining verses and see what the Bible tells us is going to happen in the last days to us and around us!

Indeed, all who delight in piety and are determined to live a devoted and godly life in Christ Jesus will meet with persecution [will be made to suffer because of their religious stand]. But wicked men and imposters will go on from bad to worse, deceiving and leading astray others and being deceived and led astray themselves. But as for you, continue to hold to the things that you have learned and of which you are convinced, knowing from whom you learned [them], and how from your childhood you have had a knowledge of and been acquainted with the sacred Writings, which are able to instruct you and give you the understanding for salvation which comes through faith in Christ Jesus [through the leaning of the entire human personality on God in Christ Jesus in absolute trust and confidence in His power, wisdom, and goodness]. Every Scripture is God-breathed (given by His inspiration) and profitable for instruction, for reproof and conviction of sin, for correction of error and discipline in obedience, [and] for training in righteousness (in holy living, in conformity to God's will in thought, purpose, and action), so that the man of God may be complete and proficient, well fitted and thoroughly equipped for every good work. 2 Timothy 3:12-17

Why must we build our foundation of Holy Spirit fruitfulness? In these last days in which we find ourselves right now, the Bible plainly tells us that when we are determined to live godly lives we will be met with persecution, and we will be made to suffer because of our stand for Christ. One must be so filled with the power and presence of the Holy Spirit that our foundation is strong, nine levels deep, and fully able to manifest through our outer court (body), our inner court (soul), and the Holy Spirit from within our Holy of Holies (spirit) living within us.

Chapter Eight
The Correlation Between the Fruit and the Gifts of the Holy Spirit

The Bible specifically lists nine gifts of the Holy Spirit that need to manifest through us for the benefit of others, and the Bible also lists nine different fruit of the Holy Spirit which is opposite of the works of the flesh. What if the fruit and the gifts of the Holy Spirit somehow work together for us? What if each level of the fruit of the Holy Spirit that is building a solid foundation within our temples is releasing the manifestation of levels of the gifts of the Holy Spirit?

Let me explain it further and maybe you will let me show you!

What if the first fruit of the Holy Spirit which we discussed in the previous chapter releases the manifestation of the first gift of the Holy Spirit? What if once we master walking in love, that the gift of the word of wisdom is released in operation within us?

Now you may be thinking what Harry brought up to me when we first discussed this topic. He said, "I have known many people over the years that manifested the gifts of the Holy Spirit but there was not much evidence of the fruit of the Holy Spirit in operation in their personal lives."

I had to agree with Harry on this point. I have known many also who operated in the gifts of the Holy Spirit, but I did not witness the fruit of the Holy Spirit in their lives either. So how can the fruit release the gifts since we both have known many people in ministry that were definitely operating in the gifts but had little to no fruit showing?

I took this to prayer and the Lord simply said, "Grace." The grace of God covers us, it's the power of God in operation to help us in our weaknesses of the flesh. Think about chapter five of Galatians. When it finally gets to the fruit of the Holy Spirit it is after many verses outlining the very opposite of the fruit of the Holy Spirit, which are the works of the flesh, or the 'fruit' of the flesh.

We have a wonderful gift that came with the forgiveness of our sins, and it is called grace. The grace of God is the power of God to continue to walk as sons and daughters of Father God even while we are still overcoming our flesh stuff.

In generations past there were many who operated strongly in the manifested gifts of the Holy Spirit, but once you knew them personally you didn't see a lot of love, joy, peace, patience, etc. flowing out of them. First of all, the gifts of the Holy Spirit are for the benefit of others, while the fruit of the Holy Spirit is for the one who is housing the Holy Spirit. Think about it.

When I am fruiting love, joy, peace, patience, kindness, goodness, faithfulness, gentleness, and self-control my personal life is doing just great! I am in a place where I can truly enjoy my life. I am not discounting the fact that when I am in this place of fruitfulness that others do not benefit! Of course, anyone who is around me enjoys the fruit of the Holy Spirit in my life. But ultimately the fruit helps me be in the right place daily, and I enjoy the benefit of it.

The gifts of the Spirit benefit others. The fruit of the Holy Spirit benefits you! The gifts of the Holy Spirit focus outward away from you to other people. The fruit of the Holy Spirit focuses inward to help you enjoy your daily walk of the Holy Spirit.

With that established let us continue to delve into how I truly believe God intends for the fruit and the gifts to flow hand in hand. I believe God's perfect plan is for us to build the foundation of our personal holy of holies within our personal temple with nine levels of foundations. With each foundation I believe God intends to release more of the gifts of the Holy Spirit to benefit others.

Again, let me reiterate. I am not dismissing the fact that many people seem to flow in the gifts without having any fruit of the Holy Spirit. But let me point out that just because we personally don't witness a person having any fruit of the Holy Spirit, that does not mean that they don't. It is not for me to judge what love, or joy, or peace, or patience looks like coming forth from another person.

I know some of the fruit of the Holy Spirit are fairly easy to see like patience or self-control, but that is based upon our measuring line of patience verses their own individual and personal measuring line before God Almighty. If I am a more naturally patient person, some people observing my life might think that I am super fruitful, when I haven't even tapped into the Holy Spirit's fruit yet, but merely my own personality showing. That is why we are warned so many times about judging others when we can never truly know what is in the heart of another person.

Let us leave all the judgment to our Father God who knows us better than we know ourselves. I don't want to plant any seeds of judgment so I won't have a harvest of judgment coming forth from what I have planted!

It certainly helps when we can see the fruit of the Holy Spirit in others. I believe it helps us receive from the other person who could be flowing in a gift of the Holy Spirit. I am thinking of so many times when people have 'given me a word' but there was no love coming forth from the giver of the word. So no matter how much I wanted to receive that word, I couldn't because of the lack of love coming forth from the giver.

Love covers a multitude of sins (and flesh). Love is the greatest gift mentioned in 1 Corinthians 13:13.

And so, faith, hope, love abide [faith-conviction and belief respecting man's relation to God and divine things; hope-joyful and confident expectation of eternal salvation; love-true affection for God and man, growing out of God's love for and in us], these three; but the greatest of these is love.

The Bible says out of the three gifts listed above, faith, hope, and love, love is the greatest! It's the very foundation of our foundations! This reminds me of the forming and preparing of the bride of Christ. The Bible uses the word foundation in the analogy of building a city called the bride.

The foundation [stones] of the wall of the city were ornamented with all of the precious stones. The first foundation [stone] was jasper, the second sapphire, the third chalcedony (or white agate), the fourth emerald, the fifth onyx, the sixth sardius, the seventh chrysolite, the eighth beryl, the ninth topaz, the tenth chrysoprase, the eleventh jacinth, the twelfth amethyst. Revelation 21:19-20

I will get to why the foundations of Christ's bride are twelve levels deep instead of nine like the fruit and the gifts of the Holy Spirit. The twelve foundations align with the divine government of the kingdom of God. The number twelve in ancient Hebrew means divine government. When Lucifer fell, he lost nine covering stones. Father gave those nine stones first to the high priest to cover the breastplate, then added another three stones for the future bride of Christ. Those three new stones added were the third row. Then we see in the twenty-first chapter of Revelation the foundation stones of the bride of Christ. She is a city with twelve stones. These are in a different order than what was listed in Exodus twenty-eight for the breastplate covering, but they are the same stones.

Nine stones were given when we take Lucifer's place on archangel level of authority, and then three more stones for the bride of Christ. I will discuss this further in a later chapter, but suffice it to say, when we accept our role given through Jesus Christ in Revelation chapter one verse six, He said that He has made us kings and priests. We, also, receive the covering of Jesus, our High Priest! This would take another book to discuss, but let me leave the thought by simply saying for you to study the Book of Hebrews, and it will become much clearer for you.

The bride of Christ submits on all levels to become His full image and authority. She has His covering and position through the power of the Holy Spirit governing her through her yielded position. Christ's bride becomes one with Christ even in His authority and position.

As I said above, it correlates with the twelve stones on the high priest's breastplate in Exodus twenty-eight. Beginning in verse seventeen you can easily see a correlation between the breastplate of the high priest and the foundations of the bride of Christ.

Remember in Revelation chapter one verse six that Jesus said He has made us kings and priests. We represent the priesthood when we are truly His bride, and our lives are no longer our own, but we are completely controlled by the Holy Spirit.

You shall set in it four rows of stones: a sardius, a topaz, and a carbuncle shall be the first row; the second row an emerald, a sapphire, and a diamond [so called at that time]; the third row a jacinth, an agate, and an amethyst; and the fourth row a beryl, an onyx, and a jasper; they shall be set in gold filigree. Exodus 28:17-20

I teach in great depth of this subject in my book Tones of the Throne Room. I want you to notice that since the number twelve means divine government that Father was making a universal heaven and earth legal decision when He set up the priesthood using the twelve stones listed in the passage of scripture above. Those same twelve stones are in the foundational stones of the bride of Christ in Revelation chapter twenty-one. Again, remember that they are in a different order. Just one point I want you to see here.

In Exodus the jasper stone is the twelfth stone, the last stone. In Revelation, the jasper stone is the first stone. Jesus Christ said of Himself, *I am the Alpha and Omega, the First and the Last (the Before all and the End of all).* Revelation 22:13

Jesus Christ had not come yet as Messiah to the earth for mankind in Exodus, but never mistake that He was not given yet. He was given! From the very beginning of the earth's re-existence, the fall of Lucifer, now Satan, Adam and Eve and the fall of humanity, God had a plan of redemption for mankind from the beginning. Jesus was given as Redeemer for mankind even before man needed a Savior!

God plans ahead! He isn't just winging it as He goes. He knows. He knows everything, everywhere, at all times. He knows before it happens because He has already been there with us! In the Book of John, we so easily can see Jesus was in the beginning. In the beginning of what? Who?

He was there. He was the Word. He was the Light. He was the Life breathed into mankind. Never ever think Jesus wasn't in the beginning. All of the triune Godhead was there. Father, Son, and Holy Spirit were triune in the beginning of what we call creation.

Now that I have taken you into the deep end of the thinking pool, let's come back to the reason for nine foundations of fruit of the Holy Spirit and nine manifestations of gifts of the Holy Spirit. What if the fruit foundations of the Holy Spirit within our human temples are the power that releases the full manifestations of the gifts of the Holy Spirit? I believe they walk hand in hand.

I believe that love helps manifest the word of wisdom. I believe that joy helps the manifestation come forth of the word of knowledge. I believe that peace brings forth the gift of faith into operation in our lives. Let's look at it where it is so easy to see the correlation between the fruit and the gifts in manifestation.

Love causes the word of wisdom to flow.
Joy causes the word of knowledge to flow.
Peace causes the gift of faith to come forth.
Patience causes the gift of healing to come forth.
Kindness causes the working of miracles to manifest.
Goodness causes the gift of prophesy to come forth.
Faithfulness causes the gift of discerning of spirits.

Gentleness releases the gift of tongues.
Self-control releases the gift of interpretation.

What if the foundation of the fruit of the Holy Spirit is what releases the long-term flow of the gifts of the Holy Spirit? It is not good enough once you have begun to flow in the gifts of the Holy Spirit to have those gifts manifest a few times and then stop flowing! Once you have experienced the flow of the gifts from within you, you will never ever want those gifts to stop flowing!

By spending time developing the fruit of the Holy Spirit in our personal lives I believe those foundations can help sustain the long-term continual flowing of the 'oil' of the gifts of the Holy Spirit. So instead of running after the manifestations of the gifts, maybe we should spend more time personally with the Holy Spirit in the secret place of our lives developing strong and sure foundations of the fruit of the Holy Spirit.

Then and only then can we be sure our eyes will remain on Jesus and our dependance upon His Holy Spirit within us. We must not get so caught up in the spectacular that we miss the supernatural. Keep building your inner foundations and watch how the manifestations of the gifts of the Holy Spirit begin to come forth one by one, stronger and stronger, as you die to self and live for Christ. Let's look at the scripture again.

Now there are distinctive varieties and distributions of endowments (gifts, extraordinary powers distinguishing certain Christians, due to the power of divine grace operating in their souls by the Holy Spirit) and they vary, but the [Holy] Spirit remains the same. And there are distinctive varieties of service and ministration, but it is the same Lord [Who is served]. And there are distinctive varieties of operation [of working to accomplish things], but it is the same God Who inspires and energizes them all in all. 1 Corinthians 12:4-6

Notice the verses say the gifts flow due to the power of divine grace operating in 'their souls by the Holy Spirit.' It is the divine grace operating in me personally that allows the Holy Spirit to begin to manifest His gifts through me for the benefit of others. As long as I am developing my inner Holy Spirit character (fruit of the Holy Spirit) I believe the divine grace grows and grows!

The moment I get my eyes on myself as 'all that and a bag of chips' then the divine grace dries up along with the operation of the gifts of the Holy Spirit. So let us continue to grow our Holy Spirit character that can help us have a long-term flow of His spiritual gifts coming forth up and out of us to help others! Remember the wife of the prophet in 2 Kings chapter four.

As long as she was willing to pour the anointing oil into empty vessels the oil continued to flow. As long as we are willing to continue to pour the oil of the Holy Spirit through us to help and benefit others who are empty and in need, the gifts will continue to flow!

To keep our eyes off of ourselves and onto the needs of others we must continue to build our Holy Spirit fruitful foundations of love, joy, peace, patience, kindness, goodness, faithfulness, gentleness, and self-control. Look one last time with the eyes of the Holy Spirit within you to watch how revelation flows into your spirit being!

Love . . . word of wisdom
Joy . . . word of knowledge
Peace . . . gift of faith
Patience . . . gift of healing
Kindness . . . working of miracles
Goodness . . . gift of prophesy
Faithfulness . . . discerning of spirits
Gentleness . . . speaking in tongues

Self-control . . . interpretation of tongues

Keep building your Holy Spirit foundations, yielding, constantly yielding to the Spirit, and watch the gifts of the Spirit begin and continue to manifest for the rest of your life for the good and benefit of others. The moment the gifts become about you, they will cease to flow.

Chapter Nine
Jesus' Relationship with the Holy Spirit

And the Holy Spirit descended upon Him in bodily form like a dove, and a voice came from heaven, saying, You are My Son, My Beloved! In You I am well pleased and find delight!
Luke 3:22

Jesus didn't begin His relationship with the Holy Spirit when the Holy Spirit anointed Him in the above verse. Jesus and the Holy Spirit were already in divine relationship as two of the triune Godhead along with Father. The above verse shows how Jesus, the Son of Man, became anointed as a human being by His newfound relationship with the Holy Spirit. He was once in Godhead-to-Godhead relationship. From this point on at around thirty years of age Jesus began His relationship with the Holy Spirit as a man.

Everything Jesus did from this point on in His life was a testimony and a sign to us of what we are capable of doing and being as humans. Jesus became the anointed Son of God fully clothed in humanity. He became Jesus Christ, the anointed

One. He fulfilled the prophetic scriptures at this pivotal point in His life to become Messiah! It was prophesied of Messiah's coming!

I will declare the decree of the Lord: He said to Me, You are My Son, this day [I declare] I have begotten You.
Psalm 2:7

Behold My Servant, Whom I uphold, My elect in Whom My soul delights! I have put My Spirit upon Him; He will bring forth justice and right and reveal truth to the nations.
Isaiah 42:1

I want to focus this chapter on Jesus' relationship with the Holy Spirit as the Son of Man. I want to show you many examples of what Jesus taught about the Holy Spirit and also how He walked fully anointed and in relationship with the Holy Spirit.

Then Jesus, full of and controlled by the Holy Spirit, returned from the Jordan and was led in [by] the [Holy] Spirit for (during) forty days in the wilderness (desert), where He was tempted (tried, tested exceedingly) by the devil. And He ate nothing during those days, and when they were completed, He was hungry. Then the devil said to Him, If You are the Son of God, order this stone to turn into a loaf [of bread]. And Jesus replied to him, It is written, man shall not live and be sustained by (on) bread alone but by every word and expression of God. Then the devil took Him up to a high mountain and showed Him all the kingdoms of the habitable world in a moment of time [in the twinkling of an eye]. And he said to Him, To You I will give all this power and authority and their glory (all their magnificence, excellence, preeminence, dignity, and grace), for it has been turned over to me, and I give it to whomever I will. Therefore, if You will do homage to and worship me [just once], it shall all be Yours. And Jesus replied to him, Get behind Me, Satan! It is written, You shall do homage to and worship the Lord your God, and Him only shall you serve. Then he took Him to Jerusalem and set Him on a gable of the temple, and said to Him, If you are the Son of God, cast Yourself down from here; For it is written, He will give His angels charge over you to guard and watch over you closely and carefully; and on their hands they will bear you up, lest you strike your foot against a stone. And Jesus replied to him, [The Scripture] says, You shall not tempt (try, test exceedingly) the Lord your God. And when the devil had ended every [the complete cycle of] temptation, he [temporarily] left Him [that is, stood off from Him] until another more opportune and favorable time. Then Jesus went back full of and under the power of the [Holy] Spirit into Galilee, and the fame of Him spread through the whole region round about. Luke 4:1-14

I realize this is a long passage of scripture but I want to establish to you the Holy Spirit's part from the very beginning of Jesus' relationship with the Holy Spirit. Jesus had lived for thirty years at this point without the divine relationship of the Holy Spirit's anointing. His cousin, John the Baptist, had just baptized Jesus, and as Jesus came up out of the water the Holy Spirit descended upon Him.

This is our first indication that the baptism of the Holy Spirit is a separate and second baptism. Once the Holy Spirit descended from heaven upon Jesus, the Father spoke and confirmed that Jesus was truly His only begotten Son. From that moment forward the Bible plainly states that Jesus was fully under the control of the Holy Spirit.

Luke chapter four actually states that Jesus was 'full of and controlled by the Holy Spirit' from that moment forward. Jesus was baptized in water, then baptized by the Holy Spirit. The Holy Spirit wasn't just with Him. The Holy Spirit was fully in Him, and Jesus had fully yielded the rest of His life to the control of the Holy Spirit.

You want to walk, talk, preach, teach, and heal like Jesus? Well, there is your formula. You must be fully filled, controlled by, and yielded to the Holy Spirit! Notice that the first act of the Holy Spirit in Jesus' life was to lead Him into the wilderness to be tempted by the devil. Uh-Oh. This might mess with your theology a bit. But I can't change the scripture to make you feel good. If you want to be like Jesus then you must accept the scripture, every verse of it, as your own. If you want to be anointed like Jesus, are you willing to allow the Holy Spirit to lead you into the desert, your very own wilderness experience, to prove your level of yieldedness to the Holy Spirit?

The Holy Spirit fully knows what the outcome of every situation is. He knew Jesus would not give in to Satan's temptation. But Jesus was fully man at this point. I suppose that when we are tested, tried, and tempted by the devil we are not proving anything to Father God. We are not proving anything to Holy Spirit. When we pass a test that is for us! That is so we can know who we are, and how yielded we really are to the Holy Spirit.

Jesus was fully controlled by the Holy Spirit while He was being tempted, tried, and tested. When you are in the worst circumstance and situation of your life, is the Holy Spirit still welcome to be with you, or do you act like He left? He did not leave; He promised He never would. But do you leave Him, when you are in trouble? If anyone separates you from the Holy Spirit, simply look in the mirror. The only one with the power to separate you from Holy Spirit is you. If you won't quit, if you won't leave, then there will never be any separation!

I propose to you, that all tests, trials, and temptations that you have gone through were never to prove anything to God. He knows everything; He knows what you will choose and what you will do even in the future! So when you are being tested, tried, and tempted those tests results are for you to know who you are! You will know when you come out of those situations if you are fully yielded to Holy Spirit. Notice when the devil was finished testing Jesus what happened next.

We can easily see that after Jesus was tested, tried, and tempted He went back to Galilee in the power of the Holy Spirit! The Holy Spirit never left Him. The Holy Spirit helped Him survive and thrive in the midst of being tempted, tried, and tested. Holy Spirit will help you! Holy Spirit helped Jesus, and He will help you! You can pass every test with flying colors and be filled with the power of the Holy Spirit.

When Jesus began to teach the disciples of the coming baptism of the Holy Spirit He was speaking from His own personal experience. That is why, I believe, He used so many adjectives to try and describe His own personal experience with the Holy Spirit. This was not His triune Godhead experience with the Holy Spirit, but His personal fully man experience with the power sent to Him from heaven. Look at the same story from Matthew's perspective.

And when Jesus was baptized, He went up at once out of the water; and behold, the heavens were opened, and he [John] saw the Spirit of God descending like a dove and alighting on Him. And behold, a voice from heaven said, This is My Son, My Beloved, in Whom I delight! Matthew 3:16-17

What I want you to notice is from where did the Holy Spirit come? He came from heaven! He came from above and SOUND, a voice, came with Holy Spirit. In Acts chapter two in the giving of Holy Spirit to mankind, the upper room was filled with the 'sound from heaven,' and a tongue of fire sat upon each humans' head. When Holy Spirit truly comes to dwell on the inside of you, the sound of heaven is heard through you! From the point you are truly baptized in the Holy Spirit and He moves from 'with you' to 'in you,' your sound changes from the sound of earth to the sound of heaven!

Let's look at Jesus' teaching on the Holy Spirit and instructing the disciples in my favorite chapter in the Bible, John chapter fourteen. As much as I want to write the whole chapter out for you I won't. I do suggest you read the whole chapter, in fact, memorize it! It is one of the most comforting and power infusing chapters in the whole Bible!

The chapter begins with Jesus confirming to His disciples that they already believe in Father God. He went on to encourage them to believe in Him, also. He talked about the future, about eternity, and what heaven is like. He assured them that if it were not like He had been telling them that He Himself would have corrected it! Jesus prepared them that He would be leaving soon and going to heaven. He told them that they would follow Him to heaven where Father had prepared a mansion for them! Thomas got all upset when Jesus said that they already knew the way to get to heaven.

I can just imagine all the disciples sitting around Jesus as He spoke of leaving them and going on to heaven. Maybe they were all in too much shock to say anything, stop Him, or even ask a question, but when Jesus stated that, 'to the place where I am going, you know the way,' Thomas just couldn't take anymore. He interrupted Jesus and let me show you the conversation.

Thomas said to Him, Lord, we do not know where You are going, so how can we know the way? Jesus said to him, I am the Way and the Truth and the Life; no one comes to the Father except by (through) Me. John 14:5

I want to stop here for a moment and point out no matter how famous a preacher is, or how many people follow him or her on Twitter, Facebook, or Instagram, or how big their tv ministry may be, or how many people attend their church services, if anyone says there is any other way to heaven other than through Jesus Christ, they are false preachers and you can't trust anything else they say. There is only one way to heaven and that is through Jesus Christ our Lord and Savior.

Let's pick up where we left off as Jesus was talking to His disciples.

If you had known Me [had learned to recognize Me], you would also have known My Father. From now on, you know Him and have seen Him. Philip said to Him, Lord, show us the Father [cause us to see the Father-that is all we ask]; then we shall be satisfied. Jesus replied, Have I been with all of you for so long a time, and do you not recognize and know Me yet, Philip? Anyone who has seen Me has seen the Father. How can you say then, Show us the Father? Do you not believe that I am in the Father, and that the Father is in Me? What I am telling you I do not say on My own authority and of My own accord; but the Father Who lives continually in Me does the (His) works (His own miracles, deeds of power).
John 14:7-10

Jesus was trying to establish to the disciples that He and Father were One, and that Father was One with Him. Before He introduced the Holy Spirit to them, He first must open their eyes to Who Father God really was to them personally.

Believe Me that I am in the Father and Father in Me; or else believe Me for the sake of the [very] works themselves. [If you cannot trust Me, at least let these works that I do in My

Father's name convince you.] I assure you, most solemnly I tell you, if anyone steadfastly believes in Me, he will himself be able to do the things that I do; and he will do even greater things than these, because I go to the Father. And I will do [I Myself will grant] whatever you ask in My Name [as presenting all that I AM], so that the Father may be glorified and extolled in (through) the Son. [Yes] I will grant [I Myself will do for you] whatever you shall ask in My Name [as presenting all that I AM]. If you [really] love Me, you will keep (obey) My commands, and I will ask the Father, and He will give you another Comforter (Counselor, Helper, Intercessor, Advocate, Strengthener, and Standby), that He may remain with you forever-The Spirit of Truth, Whom the world cannot receive (welcome, take to its heart), because it does not see Him or know and recognize Him. But you know and recognize Him, for He lives with you [constantly] and will be in you. John 14:11-17

Jesus was trying to establish first that whether they knew it or not, they had already been introduced to Father God through Jesus Christ. He told them that if they knew Jesus then they knew Father God. He downloaded so much to them in these few verses that I will spend the rest of my life trying to get the depths of this vast sermon into my spirit of thirty-one verses!

First, Jesus told them of where they would spend eternity and how to get there. Second, He dropped the bomb on them that He Himself would be leaving soon. Third, He wanted to make sure they knew Father God. Fourth, He started teaching them how to pray and to Whom to pray!

He was only beginning to try and get it all into them as He told them that if they had witnessed Him doing something that they could do that too, and even greater works than these would they do simply because I go to My Father! (Verses 12-14) By this point, I would imagine most of the disciples were on overload and could barely take any more! But Jesus was only getting started. He was determined to help them understand that the entire triune Godhead was about to be offered to them. This offer of the third person of the Godhead was not just going to be with them, like the Old Testament heroes of their faith, but soon, the very Spirit of God, the Holy Spirit, would be available to not only be with them, but to also be in them!

Jesus taught the disciples many of the depths of the available personality of the Holy Spirit through His description of His actions and operation. Jesus told them that if they really loved Him then they would keep His commandments. He went on to tell them that if 'you keep My commandments then I will know and Father will know that you really love Me.' At this point He began to move to the depth of their future relationship with the Holy Spirit. Jesus told them that He Himself would ask Father, and Father would give them Who they need to complete the mission of their lives.

Holy Spirit would come from heaven, directly from Father, and He would be so much more for them than they could imagine. Jesus told them that Holy Spirit would be their supernatural Comforter, Counselor, Helper, Intercessor, Advocate, Strengthener, and Standby. Holy Spirit will remain with you forever, Jesus told them. Jesus said that Holy Spirit is the Spirit of Truth.

Jesus told them that the world cannot receive or welcome Holy Spirit, but they would receive, welcome, know, and recognize Him. Jesus went on to tell them that they already have the Holy Spirit with them, but soon, very soon, He would move from the outside, that is, being with them, to the inside, that is fully being housed in their own spirits.

As Jesus closed out the teaching to the disciples in this particular meeting, He reiterated to them that the world would not see Him very soon, but they would see Him again.

This was Jesus reassuring them that He would appear to them after He was crucified, dead, buried and then resurrected. But I doubt if any of them actually caught on to His meaning in this one verse. (Verse nineteen)

Jesus finished His teaching to them on the Holy Spirit.

I have told you these things while I am still with you. But the Comforter (Counselor, Helper, Intercessor, Advocate, Strengthener, Standby), the Holy Spirit, Whom the Father will send in My name [in My place, to represent Me and act on My behalf], He will teach you all things. And He will cause you to recall (will remind you of, bring to your remembrance) everything I have told you. Peace I leave with you; My [own] peace I now give and bequeath to you. Not as the world gives do I give to you. Do not let your hearts be troubled, neither let them be afraid. [Stop allowing yourselves to be agitated and disturbed; and do not permit yourselves to be fearful and intimidated and cowardly and unsettled.] You heard Me tell you, I am going away and I am coming [back] to you. If you [really] loved Me, you would have been glad, because I am going to the Father; for the Father is greater and mightier than I am. And now I have told you [this] before it occurs, so that when it does take place you may believe and have faith in and rely on Me. I will not talk with you much more, for the prince (evil genius, ruler) of the world is coming. And he has no claim on Me. [He has nothing in common with Me; there is nothing in Me that belongs to him, and he has no power over Me.] But [Satan is coming and] I do as the Father has commanded Me, so that the world may know (be convinced) that I love the Father and that I do only what the Father has instructed Me to do. [I act in full agreement with His orders.] Rise, let us go away from here. John 14:25-31

Jesus taught His most beloved disciples about the Holy Spirit. He started out the teaching on Himself, and Father, and eventually finished the triune Godhead with the Holy Spirit. He continually reminded them of who they were, and what would be expected of them. He encouraged them to be all of who He had imparted into them to be. He told them that if they had seen Him do it, then they could do it too. He even took it a step further and said that they would be able to do so much more than He did.

I rather doubt if any of this made any sense at all to them, until the Holy Spirit was given on Pentecost in that upper room. Then they had the ability to 'see' what they couldn't see, and 'hear' what they had been unable to hear, and even 'understand' what their human minds were incapable of understanding! From Acts chapter two, with the giving of the Holy Spirit, and their acceptance of this Godhead representative of their beloved Jesus, their lives went from pitiful and grieving to eternal and filled with the power of God!

Acts 1:8 was the promise of, *You shall receive power when the Holy Spirit comes upon you . . .* That's exactly what happened. One hundred and twenty faithful followers of Jesus assembled together in that upper room and held on to what Jesus had promised them until it was fulfilled. They were infused with the same Spirit that raised Jesus from the dead, and they would never be the same! (Romans 8:11)

The same relationship that Jesus had with the Holy Spirit while He was on the earth has been offered to you and me. I want it! I accept Holy Spirit! I yield to Holy Spirit just as Jesus did. I want the same Spirit that raised Jesus from the dead to quicken my mortal flesh every day, and fill me to overflowing.

He who believes in Me [who cleaves to and trusts in and relies on Me] as the Scripture has said, From his innermost being shall flow [continuously] springs and rivers of living water. John 7:38

You want to be like Jesus? Receive the Holy Spirit! Jesus had already been resurrected, went to Father, and received His glorified body. He appeared to the disciples.

Then Jesus said to them again, Peace to you! [Just] as the Father has sent Me forth, so I am sending you. And having said this, He breathed on them and said to them, Receive the Holy Spirit! John 20:21-22

One of the last things Jesus said to His disciples after His resurrection was for them to 'Receive the Holy Spirit!' I would think then, that we would not mess around and not receive fully what Jesus so adamantly commanded His disciples to receive. I am asking you just as Jesus commanded, will you receive the Holy Spirit? Jesus commanded. I am asking. Holy Spirit will change you forever!

Chapter Ten
The Nature of the Spirit of God is Fire

In the next chapter we will discuss the three levels of baptism that are offered to each of us. This is such a deep revelation, and I want to elaborate on it. I was about to start that chapter, but as I began studying and praying this morning the Holy Spirit directed me to teach one chapter on the fire nature of the Spirit of God. When you see the phrase 'Spirit of God' that is referring to the Holy Spirit. Let's study the fire nature and how Father used it, uses it, and will use it to bring judgment, purity, holiness, miracles, and signs and wonders.

For You, O God, have proved us; You have tried us as silver is tried, refined, and purified. You brought us into the net (the prison fortress, the dungeon); You laid a heavy burden upon our loins. You caused men to ride over our heads [when we were prostrate], we went through fire and through water, but You brought us out into a broad, moist place [to abundance and refreshment and the open air]. I will come into Your house with burnt offerings [of entire consecration]; I will pay You my vows, which my lips uttered and my mouth promised when I was in distress. I will offer to You burnt offerings of fat lambs with rams consumed in sweet-smelling smoke; I will offer bullocks and he-goats. Selah [pause, and calmly think of that]! Psalm 66:10-15

Let's look at what Psalm sixty-six tells us about the fire nature of our God. He will try us as silver is tried. Silver is tried in fire. The silversmith puts the silver in the fire and leaves it there. He pulls it out to check it periodically. How can he tell when the silver has been purified? It's quite simple. He gazes into the silver. When he can see his reflection then he knows the silver is pure. Until he can see himself, the silver must go back into the fire. When God is purifying us, He allows us to be put into His fire and we remain there, until we become His reflection. Once He can see Himself in us, then and only then, does He pull us out of the fire. Then and only then are we pure enough to reflect Him only.

Whether we will ever accept it or not, God's nature is fire, and when we run to Him, we run to His fire to purify and perfect us to be His image, and not a mixture of ourselves and Himself. We, in ourselves, are not pure. He is always pure. His best for us is to be purified with 'self' burned out of us; only His nature should remain.

Fire is God's nature. Fire is the Spirit of God's nature.

Fire goes before Him and burns up His adversaries on all sides. Psalm 97:3 *(AMP)*

For our God [is indeed] a consuming fire. Hebrews 12:29

For the Lord your God is a consuming fire, a jealous God. Deuteronomy 4:24

The nature of our God is fire, not just any kind of fire, but a consuming fire.

Know therefore this day that the Lord your God is He Who goes over before you as a devouring fire. He will destroy them and bring them down before you; so you shall dispossess them and make them perish quickly, as the Lord has promised you.
Deuteronomy 9:3

The very nature of God is fire.

Fire goes before Him and burns up His adversaries round about. His lightnings illumine the world; the earth sees and trembles. The hills melted like wax at the presence of the Lord, at the presence of the Lord of the whole earth. The heavens declare His righteousness, and all the peoples see His glory.
Psalm 97:3-6

The Strong's Concordance gives us a deeper look into the descriptive word used to describe the kind of fire that our God is. The word is 'consuming.' The Strongs number for it is H398. It is the Hebrew word 'akal' pronounced 'aw-kal.' It is defined as a primitive root; to eat (literally or figuratively): - X at {all} burn {up} {consume} devour {-er} {up} {dine} eat ({-er} {up}) feed ({with}) X {freely} X in . . . wise ({-deed} {plenty}) (lay) {meat} X quite. This word occurs 810 times throughout the Bible in 701 different verses.

Continuing to use the Strong's Concordance I further researched the word 'fire'. It is the Hebrew word 'esh' and is pronounced 'aysh'. It is the Strong's number H784 occurring 380 times in 348 verses in the Bible. The definition is a primitive word; fire (literally or figuratively):-{burning} {fiery} {fire} {flaming} hot. In the KJV the uses are for fire, burning, fiery, untranslated variants, fire, flaming, and hot.

I hope you have read and studied our books on marriage, Two Becoming One and Don't Kill Each Other; Let God Do It! Within these two books you will find the exhaustive study we have done on male and female and how mankind was created as one human being, and later separated into two beings, male and female.

In the ancient Hebrew language, within the definitions of both male and female you find this same 'esh' fire. Male means 'his hand is in the midst of the (esh) fire.' Female means 'what comes out of the (esh) fire.'

From this study you can easily see how God put Himself in both male and female to bring about cleansing and purity from within us. He made a place for the baptism of fire that we must choose to walk as His image. He made a way for us to be His image through the acceptance of His fire within us. It has always been, and it always will be our choice whether or not to accept His fire within our beings, making us eternal 'fire creatures.' The other choice is to stay earthly, human, fleshly. As far as I am concerned that is no choice at all.

God has coded within our very DNA from our mother's womb, even from the very creation of humanity through Adam, (Genesis 5:1 'and He named them both Adam') the ability to walk as His fire creatures. We have been given the ability to be filled with God's fire nature when we choose to allow His fire to live within us!

If you noticed the definition of the two words placed together, consuming fire, in ancient Hebrew means 'strong devourer.' God goes before us as a strong devourer, burning up the enemy that would try and devour us! God is a supernatural eternal 'back fire' to the demonic fires that would try and consume us! God sets a back fire before me and burns up my enemies!

God's fire nature has always been for us, not against us. His fire nature is to help us be and stay purified. Only when we resist God's nature do we find ourselves consumed by what was meant to help us. Resisting God and His nature only prolongs the process of purification and eventually, if we never submit to the process, we will spend eternity in the 'lake of fire' instead of being cleansed by God's fire nature.

Don't resist what was meant to be for us! Don't resist purification. Resisting purification only brings eternal judgment which God never intended for us. The lake of fire was created for the devil, not for humanity.

Then He will say to those at His left hand, Begone from Me, you cursed, into the eternal fire prepared for the devil and his angels! Matthew 25:41

Many people will spend an eternity in a place that was not prepared for them! Eternal fire was prepared for the devil and his demons, but humans that refuse the purifying fire of God's nature will have to spend eternity in a judgment damned fire not even prepared for them in the first place. Make sure you are not resisting the fire of God today, for eternity is a very long time. We have too many instances throughout the Bible where God had to use fire as judgment when it should have been used for cleansing purification.

The devil hates fire because that's where he started, and it's where he will end up. Instead of accepting the purification of God's fire his pride lifted him up out of God's fire and caused his future to change immediately. Ezekiel twenty-eight and Isaiah fourteen give us detailed descriptions of the fall of Lucifer. All of Isaiah fourteen is very enlightening as to the details of both, generations of antichrist spirits (kings of Babylon), and the first antichrist, Lucifer himself.

The Lord has broken the staff of the wicked, the scepter of the [tyrant] rulers, who smote the peoples in anger with incessant blows and trod down the nations in wrath with unrelenting persecution-[until] he who smote is persecuted and no one hinders any more. The whole earth is at rest and is quiet; they break forth into singing. Yes, the fir trees and cypresses rejoice at you [O kings of Babylon], even the cedars of Lebanon, saying, Since you have been laid low, no woodcutter comes up against us. Sheol (Hades, the place of the dead) below is stirred up to meet you at your coming [O tyrant Babylonian rulers]; it stirs up the shades of the dead to greet you-even all the chief ones of the earth; it raises from their thrones [in astonishment at your humbled condition] all the kings of the nations. All of them will [tauntingly] say to you, Have you also become weak as we are? Have you become like us? Your pomp and magnificence are brought down to Sheol (the underworld), along with the sound of your harps; the maggots [which prey upon dead bodies] are spread out under you and worms cover you [O Babylonian rulers]. How have you fallen from heaven, O light-bringer and daystar, son of the morning! How you have been cut down to the ground, you who weakened and laid low the nations [O blasphemous, satanic king of Babylon!]. And you said in your heart, I will ascend to heaven; I will exalt my throne above the stars of God; I will sit upon the mount of assembly in the uttermost north. I will ascend above the heights of the clouds; I will make myself like the Most High. Yet you shall be brought down to Sheol (Hades), to the innermost recesses of the pit (the region of the dead). Those who see you will gaze at you and consider you, saying, Is this the man who made the earth tremble, who shook kingdoms?-Who made the world like a wilderness and overthrew its cities, who would not permit his prisoners to return home? All the kings of the nations, all of them lie sleeping in glorious array, each one in his own sepulcher. But you are cast away from your tomb like a loathed growth or premature birth or an abominable branch [of the family] and like the raiment of the slain; and you are clothed with the slain, those thrust through with the sword, who go down to the stones of the pit [into which carcasses are thrown], like a dead body

trodden underfoot. You shall not be joined with them in burial, because you have destroyed your land and have slain your people. May the descendants of evildoers nevermore be named! Prepare a slaughtering place for his sons because of the guilt and iniquity of their fathers, so that they may not rise, possess the earth, and fill the face of the world with cities. And I will rise up against them, says the Lord of hosts, and cut off from Babylon name and remnant, and son and son's son, says the Lord. I will also make it a possession of the hedgehog and porcupine, and of marshes and pools of water, and I will sweep it with the broom of destruction, says the Lord of hosts. The Lord of hosts has sworn, saying, Surely, as I have thought and planned, so shall it come to pass, and as I have purposed, so shall it stand-That I will break the Assyrian in My land, and upon My mountains I will tread him underfoot. Then shall the [Assyrian's] yoke depart from [the people of Judah], and his burden depart from their shoulders. This is the [Lord's] purpose that is purposed upon the whole earth [regarded as conquered and put under tribute by Assyria], and this is [His omnipotent] hand that is stretched out over all the nations. For the Lord of hosts has purposed, and who can annul it? And His hand is stretched out, and who can turn it back?
Isaiah 14:5-23

I realize this is a very long passage of scripture and in referencing the fall of Lucifer it is not generally all used. But not only did I want you to see the passage of scripture giving descriptions of the fall of the light-bearer, and the son of the morning, not only did I want you to see his big speech on the five 'I wills,' but also the full address to the generations of 'kings of Babylon' which I believe are in reference to the many antichrist spirits that have embodied prideful humanity.

Notice that God has His final say so, His final thoughts and purposes will be fulfilled! And ultimately, when you understand that God is in our past, present, and future all at the same time you realize that this is already finished for every antichrist spirit, demon possessed human, and the very fallen Lucifer, the devil himself!

Now let's look at Ezekiel as more descriptive details of Lucifer's fall from his very high position as archangel of worship under the Godhead leadership of the Holy Spirit. We will discuss this in the chapter on The Hierarchy of the Kingdom of God.

Son of man, take up a lamentation over the king of Tyre and say to him, Thus says the Lord God: You are the full measure and pattern of exactness [giving the finishing touch to all that constitutes completeness], full of wisdom and perfect in beauty. You were in Eden, the garden of God, every precious stone was your covering, the carnelian, topaz, jasper, chrysolite, beryl, onyx, sapphire, carbuncle, and emerald; and your settings and your sockets and engravings were wrought in gold. On the day that you were created they were prepared. You were the anointed cherub that covers with overshadowing [wings], and I set you so. You were upon the holy mountain of God; you walked up and down in the midst of the stones of fire [like the paved work of gleaming sapphire stone upon which the God of Israel walked on Mount Sinai]. You were blameless in your ways from the day you were created until iniquity and guilt were found in you. Through the abundance of your commerce you were filled with lawlessness and violence, and you sinned; therefore I cast you out as a profane thing from the mountain of God and the guardian cherub drove you out from the midst of the stones of fire. Your heart was proud and lifted up because of your beauty; you corrupted your wisdom for the sake of your splendor. I cast you to the ground; I lay you before kings, that they might gaze at you. You have profaned your sanctuaries by the multitude of your iniquities and the enormity of your guilt, by the unrighteousness of your trade. Therefore I have brought forth a fire from your midst; it has consumed you, and I have reduced you to ashes upon the earth in the sight of all who looked at you. All who know you among the people are astonished and appalled at you; you have come to a horrible end and shall never return to being. Ezekiel 28:12-19

I'm sure as you were reading the passage of scripture that you noticed that God created him, and set him in the midst of the stones of fire. He was given the authority to walk back and forth in God's fiery stones. He was covered in beauty and music came forth from his inner being. But he turned. He turned his worship from God to himself.

He became a navel gazer and was consumed with himself, much like the culture of today. His choice caused him to be thrown out of the mountain of God. He lost his place in the midst of the stones of fire. He wanted to be like God, and then God replaced him with humanity. We are the very image of God, but only when we stay in the fire of God! We were created with the ability to be the very image of God, but when we resist God's fire nature, we are not His image, and we do not have access to His throne.

Only those who embrace the fire of God's nature are purified enough to be His image. Only those who run into God's fire nature come out purified and made holy.

Think about the three Hebrew young men in Daniel chapter three. This is one of those kings of Babylon to whom Isaiah fourteen was referring. Nebuchadnezzar had set up an idol image of himself and declared that all who would not worship the golden image would be 'thrown into the midst of a burning fiery furnace.'

Shadrach, Meshach, and Abednego refused to bow down, and the evil king had them thrown into the fire. One of my favorite speeches given in Daniel was done so by one of these teenage young men.

O Nebuchadnezzar, it is not necessary for us to answer you on this point. If our God Whom we serve is able to deliver us from the burning fiery furnace, He will deliver us out of your hand, O king. But if not, let it be known to you, O king, that we will not serve your gods or worship the golden image which you have set up! Daniel 3:16-18

The king was furious and had them thrown into the fire. But they were not resisting the fire, in truth, our God literally became the fire in which they were thrown! Our God is an all-consuming fire!

Our God is not afraid of the world's fires. Our God is not afraid of the enemies' fires. Our God is not intimidated by the devil or any of his antichrist demon possessed humans' threats against us!

He simply will become the very fire that the enemy means to use to destroy us! God sets a heavenly back fire and devours the devil's fire! Those three Hebrew boys were having so much fun in God's fire because Jesus, the true fire walker, was in Father's fire with them!

I can just imagine when the king called them to come out of his fire, that they didn't hurry to get out. I can just imagine them saying, "It's safer in here within God's fire than it is out there with you!" Sometimes I wonder if we could experience God at a much higher and even deeper level of Who He is, if we would trust Him enough to run into the fire instead of being so afraid to have to go through anything.

Too many Christians say they have the Holy Spirit but they have no fire. Fire speaks life only. Fire of God never speaks death! A death and defeated speaking tongue is an unbaptized tongue! The ability to destroy your enemies depends on the temperature of your fire.

Look at Lot's wife. In Genesis we see a story of God sending judgment to an entire region, two cities to be exact, Sodom and Gomorrah. He sent two destroyer angels to wipe out both cities with fire because of the sin and abomination found there. Abraham had taken the situation to God's court and petitioned for a stay of execution.

He petitioned the court to hold off the judgment of fire if he could produce ten righteous men. But there were not ten righteous men so the judgment fire execution order stayed in place. The destroyer angels went into the city to bring out the only righteous man and his family before the fire judgment happened.

Lot, his wife, and two daughters were led away from the city as the fire began to fall. They were all warned to not look back.

And when they had brought them forth, they said, Escape for your life! Do not look behind you or stop anywhere in the whole valley; escape to the mountains [of Moab], lest you be consumed. And Lot said to them, Oh, not that, my lords! Behold now, your servant has found favor in your sight, and you have magnified your kindness and mercy to me in saving my life; but I cannot escape to the mountains, lest the evil overtake me, and I die. See now yonder city; it is near enough to flee to, and it is a little one. Oh, let me escape to it! Is it not a little one? And my life will be saved! And [the angel] said to him, See, I have yielded to your entreaty concerning this thing also; I will not destroy this city of which you have spoken. Make haste and take refuge there, for I cannot do anything until you arrive there. Therefore, the name of the city was called Zoar [little]. The sun had risen over the earth when

Lot entered Zoar. Then the Lord rained on Sodom and on Gomorrah brimstone and fire from the Lord out of the heavens. He overthrew, destroyed, and ended those cities, and all the valley and all the inhabitants of the cities, and what grew on the ground. But [Lot's] wife looked back from behind him, and she became a pillar of salt. Genesis 19:17-26

The whole family was rescued from the judgment fire and given only one instruction to be saved. Don't look back. They were already safe in the little town of Zoar and the destroying angels had begun raining the judgment fire on the region. Then we see the little word that can change everything. But Lot's wife looked back, and she was judged because of her disobedience. How many times has the Holy Spirit warned you not to look back? How many times has God's grace covered you in your disobedience? Are you willing to bet that the last time wasn't the last time? If I were you, I would listen to the Holy Spirit, and never look back at your past again.

Lot and his family were rescued from the last move of God, and were given the privilege to be a huge part of the next move of God! Lot's wife looked back and lost the honor of it. She was created to be a fire starter in the next big move of God, but instead, she became a monument to the last move of God. God is moving forward. If you look back you could miss your opportunity to be in the next move of God's presence!

We are created to go from 'glory to glory,' but if you can't stop looking at what was, you will miss what is happening through God's power and glory right now! Looking back can bring about God's judgment fire upon our lives quicker than anything else. Be careful; listen and obey quickly. Don't wait around for the Holy Spirit to give you more instructions or explain the plan of God. He owes us no explanations. We are privates in the army of God, given orders by Commander and Chief. He doesn't have to run it by us! And He won't.

You will either obey and walk in the power and authority of God, or you will disobey and be caught in the fire of God's judgment.

He can either be the back fire that turns the devil's destruction away from you, or He can be the very judgment upon your life because of your disobedience. Even if you are the biggest gambler on earth, I suspect, your luck has run out. Don't try or test our God. He is an all-consuming fire, and He is jealous for your undivided attention.

Let me finish this chapter with the scriptures about the lake of fire. We can either embrace the fire of God when He is offering that purifying, cleansing fire, or we can suffer the rest of eternity in a lake of fire that was not created for humanity.

And the beast was seized and overpowered, and with him the false prophet who in his presence had worked wonders and performed miracles by which he led astray those who had accepted or permitted to be placed upon them the stamp (mark) of the beast and those who paid homage and gave divine honors to his statue. Both of them were hurled alive into the fiery lake that burns and blazes with brimstone. Revelation 19:20

And that's the end of the beast and the false prophet.

Then the devil who had led them astray [deceiving and seducing them] was hurled into the fiery lake of burning brimstone, where the beast and false prophet were; and they will be tormented day and night forever and ever (through the ages of the ages). Revelation 20:10

Now we know where the devil, the beast, and the false prophet will spend eternity. The devil hates fire; it reminds him of his future! When we are on fire for God, filled with the Holy

Spirit and His fire, we remind the devil of what is coming for him!

Then death and Hades (the state of death or disembodied existence) were thrown into the lake of fire. This is the second death, the lake of fire. Revelation 20:14

And that's the verdict on death and hell.

And if anyone's [name] was not found recorded in the Book of Life, he was hurled into the lake of fire. Revelation 20:15

It's not good enough for you to know Him; He had better know you! He had better know you so well that your name is recorded in His book! Contrary to popular belief, everybody is not going to heaven.

People who followed the devil here on earth, will follow the devil for eternity, right into the lake of fire. They don't even get to go to hell for eternity; they have to spend eternity in the lake of fire!

But as for the cowards and the ignoble and the contemptible and the cravenly lacking in courage and the cowardly submissive, and as for the unbelieving and faithless, and as for the depraved and defiled with abominations, and as for murderers and the lewd and adulterous and the perceivers of magic arts and the idolaters (those who give supreme devotion to anyone or anything other than God) and all liars (those who knowingly convey untruth by word or deed)-[all of these shall have] their part in the lake that blazes with fire and brimstone. This is the second death. Revelation 21:8

That just about wraps it up for who will spend eternity in the lake of fire which the Bible repeatedly calls 'the second death.' What a list that one is!

1. Cowards
2. Ignoble
3. Contemptible
4. Cravenly lacking in courage
5. Cowardly submissive
6. Unbelieving
7. Faithless
8. Depraved
9. Defiled with abominations
10. Murderers
11. Lewd
12. Adulterous
13. Perceivers of magic arts
14. Idolaters
15. Liars

If you find yourself anywhere on that list, stop right now and repent. Get on your knees and repent before God for I do not want you to spend eternity in the lake of fire! Jesus is the only way to heaven!

There is a fire that is for you! It's God's fire nature! Jesus was a fire walker in Daniel three. The three Hebrew boys became fire walkers. Lucifer was created to be a fire walker, but he went from perfect from the day he was created to cast out of God's fire nature doomed for the lake of fire for all of eternity.

Elijah was a fire prophet. Three captains came before Elijah. Elijah was God's prophet to the nation. Elijah was a fire walker and a fire starter. Notice what happened to the first two captains because they did not respect the prophet of God, nor did they respect the fire of God.

Elijah said to the captain of fifty, If I am a man of God, then let fire come down from heaven and consume you and your fifty. And fire fell from heaven and consumed him and his fifty. Again King [Ahaziah] sent to him another captain of fifty with his fifty. And he said to Elijah, Man of God, the king has said, Come down quickly! And Elijah answered, If I am a man of God, let fire come down from heaven and consume you and your fifty. And the fire of God came down from heaven and consumed him and his fifty. Ahaziah sent again a captain of a third fifty with his fifty. And the third captain of fifty went up and fell on his knees before Elijah and besought him and said to him. O man of God, I pray you, let my life and life of these fifty, your servants, be precious in your sight. Behold, fire came down from heaven and burned up the two captains of the former fifties with their fifties. Therefore let my life now be precious in your sight. 2 Kings 1:10-14

The third captain not only respected the prophet but also the fire of God. He and his men were spared because he bowed his knee and accepted the fire of God.

God's nature is fire. We can either embrace the nature of God and our lives will be purified and made ready, (we will become His image) or we can spend eternity regretting what we didn't do while here on earth. When Moses first encountered the Spirit of God, he witnessed a bush on fire and not being burned up.

The Angel of the Lord appeared to him in a flame of fire out of the midst of a bush; and he looked, and behold, the bush burned with fire, yet was not consumed. And Moses said, I will now turn aside and see this great sight, why the bush is not burned. And when the Lord saw that he turned aside to see, God called to him out of the midst of the bush and said, Moses, Moses! And he said, Here am I. God said, Do not come near; put your shoes off your feet, for the place on which you stand is holy ground. Exodus 3:2-4

Later on in Moses' journey with the Spirit of God he was on the mountain. The finger of God wrote the Ten Commandments on tablets, and Moses had them to bring down to the people. The Lord warned him to hurry and get down there because the people were corrupting themselves. The conversation continued between the Spirit of God and Moses.

As Moses came down the mountain he turned and looked back at it.

So I turned and came down from the mountain, and the mountain was burning with fire. And the two tables of the covenant were in my two hands. Deuteronomy 9:15

Where the Spirit of God is fire remains. We can either yield to the fire of God's Spirit or we can be burned up by it. I have determined to yield to God's Spirit nature and be a spirit fire walker all the days of my life.

When our daughter went to heaven many years ago, Father gave me many revelations that helped me continue to move forward. One such revelation came in a statement after much prayer. The Spirit of God said to me, "The earth and your time here is like the womb of heaven. You were sent to earth to develop into who you will be for eternity." Don't waste your womb time; develop into the eternal image of God you are created to be. Father, send Your fire! I lay myself on Your altar as a sacrifice.

Let me now show you how the Holy Spirit is the fire of God inside of your very being. Let me show you how your natural nature can be consumed by God's fire nature through the power of the Holy Spirit. If you have the courage, let's go to the next chapter!

Chapter Eleven
Three Baptisms: Water, Holy Spirit, and Fire

I indeed baptize you in (with) water because of repentance [that is, because of your changing your minds for the better, heartily amending your ways, with abhorrence of your past sins]. But He Who is coming after me is mightier than I, Whose sandals I am not worthy or fit to take off or carry; He will baptize you with the Holy Spirit and with fire.
Matthew 3:11

John the Baptist, was talking to his followers. He was born to Elizabeth and Zachariah. Zachariah was a priest, and Elizabeth was Mary's cousin. Yes, Mary, the mother of Jesus, was a cousin to John's mother. So since I am from Mississippi you have to know what I am about to say! That makes Jesus and John third cousins. They must have grown up together. John was six months older than Jesus.

His entire purpose of being on the earth was to be the forerunner of Messiah. He would announce the coming of the Lord! His very words transcend time as he boldly proclaimed,

Look! There is the Lamb of God, Who takes away the sin of the world! Look! There is the Lamb of God! John 1:29, 36

John knew who his cousin was! He was bold, born into the lineage of priesthood, and he was not afraid to tell everyone that Jesus was Messiah! But even John's words from the beginning of Jesus' ministry were prophetic of the coming crucifixion as John called Jesus, the sacrificial Lamb of God!

John was a true prophet. He was filled with the Holy Spirit even in his mother's womb . . . *and he will be filled with and controlled by the Holy Spirit even in and from his mother's womb.* Luke 1:15b

He never seemed concerned with pleasing people, or even remotely interested in 'saying the right thing.' His words were never to tickle one's ears or make the hearer feel good about oneself. His whole purpose was to reveal Messiah and bring repentance to mankind. His ministry revolved around turning people from going the wrong way to helping them through repentance to go the way of Jesus, the Messiah.

His words cut the hearts of those around him in his lifetime, and his words still cry out today. *Repent (think differently; change your mind, regretting your sins and changing your conduct), for the kingdom of heaven is at hand.* Matthew 3:2

John fulfilled his purpose. He obeyed the Spirit of God that led him and because he obeyed, he knew what others did not seem to grasp. His cousin was the long-awaited Messiah! Isaiah prophesied about Jesus and His coming, but Isaiah also prophesied about John.

A voice of one who cries: Prepare in the wilderness the way of the Lord [clear away the obstacles]; make straight and smooth in the desert a highway for our God! Isaiah 40:3

John's ministry made the way for Jesus' ministry to follow. It is no surprise then that John as priest was the only one qualified to baptize Jesus. Make no mistake about it. When Jesus laid His life down on the river bank and waded into the water to be baptized, from the moment He came out of the water His life was forever turned.

If you were water baptized but your life did not make a dramatic change from that day forth, you need to examine your heart and your salvation. You need to make a commitment once again, lay your pride down on the edge of the riverbank and wade into the water.

Really allow your life to be fully immersed in His presence. Allow the washing of the water to be the outward sign of an inward change. When you come up out of the water, listen for the voice of your Father God to speak to you.

Then Jesus came from Galilee to the Jordan to John to be baptized by him. But John protested strenuously, having in mind to prevent Him, saying, It is I who have need to be baptized by You, and do You come to me? But Jesus replied to him, Permit it just now; for it is the fitting way for [both of] us to fulfill all righteousness [that is, to perform completely whatever is right]. Then he permitted Him. And when Jesus was baptized, He went up at once out of the water; and behold, the heavens were opened, and he [John] saw the Spirit of God descending like a dove and alighting on Him. And behold, a voice from heaven said, This is My Son, My Beloved, in Whom I delight! Matthew 3:13-17

Jesus knew to fulfill His purpose as the Son of Man, that He must be water baptized. But notice what happened next for Jesus! John witnessed the next baptism for Jesus! John saw the Spirit of God, the Holy Spirit, descending like a dove and alighting on Jesus! Once Jesus received the Holy Spirit, then the voice from heaven was heard! This particular voice was the voice of Father! Father approved His Son, and baptized Jesus with the Holy Spirit!

From that point on in Jesus' life the Holy Spirit was with Him, and the Holy Spirit led Him. He immediately was led by the Holy Spirit into the wilderness to be tempted by the devil. When those tests, trials, and temptations were finished the Holy Spirit was still with Jesus.

Jesus went back full of and under the power of the [Holy] Spirit into Galilee, and the fame of Him spread through the whole region round about. Luke 4:14

Jesus began teaching and preaching in the synagogues full of the Holy Spirit and His power! He traveled around and preached, and taught all who would listen even in Nazareth. He prophesied about Himself using the scrolls from Isaiah sixty-one and then announced that the scriptures had been fulfilled.

Once Jesus was filled and controlled by the Holy Spirit He preached, taught, cast out devils, and healed with authority, ability, weight and power! When you receive the baptism of the Holy Spirit your life becomes filled with the power of God!

But you shall receive power (ability, efficiency, and might) when the Holy Spirit has come upon you, and you shall be My witnesses in Jerusalem and all Judea and Samaria and to the ends (the very bounds) of the earth. Acts 1:8

This was the very last thing Jesus said to His followers before He ascended into heaven. Then angels followed up Jesus' instructions with these words.

Men of Galilee, why do you stand gazing into heaven? This

same Jesus, Who was caught away and lifted up from among you into heaven, will return in [just] the same way in which you saw Him go into heaven. Acts 1:11

With their instructions they journeyed into Jerusalem. It took them three days to get there. Then they made their way up the stairs to the upper room where they stayed as they waited. They had no idea how long they were to wait. They didn't know when the Holy Spirit would come, but they knew He would come! They had been told to wait for the Holy Spirit so they waited. The key to receiving from heaven is not in the promise of what is to come, but the key to receiving from heaven is in 'how' you wait!

The Bible tells us in Acts that they were in full agreement and they all devoted themselves to steadfastly pray until Holy Spirit was given to them. How many times do we say we will pray but once it takes a while, once the promise doesn't come right away, we give up and go home. This group was not leaving without the fulfillment of the promise of the Holy Spirit and His power!

While they prayed over the course of the next few days, they also took care of some ministry business. They needed a replacement for Judas. Two men were nominated to take Judas' place, Joseph called Barsabbas, who was surnamed, Justus, and Matthias. They all prayed, and they all sought the Lord as to the right choice. Then they drew lots. Yes, that's what the scripture said. They basically drew names. Why? Because the Holy Spirit had not been given to them yet, and they didn't have His leading. So they drew lots! Matthias' name was chosen from the hat, and he became the replacement disciple.

Aren't you thankful we now have the Holy Spirit to lead us? I am thanking Father right now for the giving of the Holy Spirit to help us, lead us, guide us, assure us, advocate for us, stand in the gap before the Righteous Judge for us, and so much more Holy Spirit does for us!

And when the day of Pentecost had fully come, they were all assembled together in one place, when suddenly there came a sound from heaven like the rushing of a violent tempest blast, and it filled the whole house in which they were sitting. And there appeared to them tongues resembling fire, which were separated and distributed and which settled on each one of them. And they were all filled (diffused throughout their souls) with the Holy Spirit and began to speak in other (different, foreign) languages (tongues), as the Spirit kept giving them clear and loud expression [in each tongue in appropriate words]. Acts 2:1-4

If you have followed my ministry over the years, or read any of my books, you may have heard me teach on this revelation. I want you to notice that the writer of the book of Acts was trying to express in natural words a very supernatural happening. He searched for descriptive words to try and describe this event. I am sure you have heard the old saying, 'You just should have been there!' Well, I am fairly certain that phrase would most definitely apply to this event!

In considering the three levels of baptism spoken of by John in Matthew chapter three, I want you to notice the giving of the final two baptisms in the above scriptures. I want you to notice that the baptism of the Holy Spirit and the baptism of fire are two separate baptisms, and both come from heaven.

The first very descriptive phrase and the most misinterpreted I believe is 'suddenly there came a sound from heaven.' Let's just stop right there. What came from heaven? There came a SOUND from heaven. As the writer was trying to describe how an entire room could be immediately and suddenly filled with sound, he used the phrase 'like the rushing of a violent tempest blast.'

The room was not filled with a violent tempest blast. That was the writer's descriptive phrase to try and explain how sound could fill the room all at once! It was like a massive wind storm filled every inch of this room! You wouldn't believe it! Sound was everywhere! It wasn't earth's sound. It was heaven's sound, and they were all permeated with it! SOUND from heaven filled the whole room!

The first baptism was water. Jesus convinced John to water baptize Him. The second baptism was the sound of heaven, and it filled them. That is the infilling of the Holy Spirit's baptism. Your sound changes from the sound of earth to the sound of heaven. Holy Spirit does not move inside of you to leave you the same way He found you. The first thing He does is change your sound!

Isaiah was the prophet to the nation. That was his job, his profession, his calling. He was the sound of heaven to the king and to the people of the nation. His uncle was the king and he died. Let's pick up the story and read it from the Bible.

In the year that King Uzziah died, [in a vision] I saw the Lord sitting upon a throne, high and lifted up, and the skirts of His train filled the [most holy part of the] temple. Above Him stood the seraphim; each had six wings: with two [each] covered his [own] face, and with two [each] covered his feet, and with two [each] flew. And one cried to another and said, Holy, holy, holy is the Lord of hosts; the whole earth is full of His glory! And the foundations of the thresholds shook at the voice of him who cried, and the house was filled with smoke. Then said I, Woe is me! For I am undone and ruined, because I am a man of unclean lips, and I dwell in the midst of a people of unclean lips; for my eyes have seen the King, the Lord of hosts! Then flew one of the seraphim [heavenly beings] to me, having a live coal in his hand which he had taken with tongs from off the altar; and with it he touched my mouth and said, Behold, this has touched your lips; your iniquity and guilt are taken away, and your sin is completely atoned for and forgiven. Also I heard the voice of the Lord, saying, Whom shall I send? And who will go for Us? Then said I, Here am I; send me. Isaiah 6:1-8

I have inserted this story because I want you to see what changed the sound of Isaiah the prophet. His whole life was in the sound coming out of his mouth. He and his wife were both prophets. History tells us that they were a couple and, at times, prophesied together as husband and wife. But here, Isaiah is alone in the presence of God.

When the story starts out that his uncle, the king, had died, it makes me wonder if he is in mourning and grief. It makes me wonder if he is concerned about his job as the national prophet. One thing about it, he was searching for an answer from the Lord, and the Lord took him into a vision to answer his soul's search.

First the Lord showed Isaiah Himself as King of kings and Lord of lords. He showed Him what He looks like and Who He is! He heard the angelic creatures crying out in worship. Holy, holy, holy is the Lord! The whole earth is filled with His glory.

First, he saw the vision. He saw the Lord! He saw the angels. Then he heard the worship and the declarations of the angels. The whole earth is filled with His glory! Then he felt an earthquake, and with it came the conviction of what was wrong with his life. The Shekinah glory of the Holy Spirit filled the whole temple! And Isaiah knew immediately what was wrong with his life. His words were 'Woe is me! For I am undone and ruined, because I am a man of unclean lips.'

In the presence of the Spirit of God, the Holy Spirit, he knew immediately that his words were not acceptable for a man of God! When will we accept the conviction from the Holy Spirit that we must change our sound from the sound of earth to the sound of heaven?

Isaiah knew it. You may spend your whole life trying to clean yourself up and make yourself good enough to be in God's presence only to fail each and every time. But one moment in the presence of the Spirit of God, the Holy Spirit, and you know what to do. Repent. Isaiah repented of his own words. He said my words are unclean. He went on to say that he was surrounded by a people who all talked just like he did.

God's 'coal of fire' changed his tongue and his words. If the devil doesn't feel the heat of God's fire coming out of your mouth when he gets around you, you aren't baptized in God's fire. Once he confessed that he had unclean lips, wrong talk, he repented. The word repent in ancient Hebrew does not have the same meaning as it does in our current culture. In ancient Hebrew the word repent means 'to burn the house to the ground.' What? Let me explain. In the ancient language many words had deeper meanings than a simple surface definition. Repent is one of those words.

The word picture, or story that was used to fully define the word was this. Let's say a city was captured by an enemy. The enemy rounded up all the people from the city and took them away. As they left and were far enough away to still see their home, they were made to turn around and watch while their captors burned their homes to the ground.

Repentance to God is not merely feeling bad about your past, or even about saying you are sorry and asking for forgiveness.

True repentance means you trust God enough to allow the fire of His presence to burn your past to the ground as if it never existed. Lot's wife did not repent of her sin, but rather, she longed to return to it, and was burned up!

When Isaiah repented before the Lord of his unclean lips, it was a burning to the ground of his prior words even as the prophet to the nation. It was a yielding to the fire of the Spirit of God to change his words forever. He yielded his tongue to the coal of fire. He opened his mouth and yielded his speech, his sound, his words, and yes, even his prophesy to the fire of the Holy Spirit. He was forgiven and completely clean.

Isaiah started this story with 'woe is me' and ended it with 'Lord, send me!' What happened in the middle? The fire of God touched his tongue. If your mouth speaks death and defeat then you have an unbaptized tongue!

Go back to Acts chapter two. First, the sound of heaven filled the room in which they were sitting. Then there appeared to them tongues. They heard the sound of heaven, and saw tongues. Let me say that again. They heard the sound of heaven, and then they saw tongues. Not just any tongues, did they see. They saw tongues that looked like fire. They saw fire tongues. They saw tongues of fire. They saw tongues on fire.

I can't help but stop and point out here, that they 'saw' tongues. The Bible doesn't say that they heard tongues. It plainly says that they saw tongues. Let me propose to you that until you receive the 'sound of heaven' instead of your constant receiving of the 'sound of earth,' you won't see fire tongues.

This was two separate events happening on the day of Pentecost. Why were they celebrating this big holiday called

Pentecost? The Jews believed that was the weekend that Moses received the Ten Commandments.

Remember when the mountain was on fire? Yes, Pentecost was the national celebration of the Word given to God's people. On the same holiday thousands of years later, the Holy Spirit was given to God's people!

John the Baptist, spoke of three separate baptisms: water, Holy Spirit, and fire. We have the giving of both the Holy Spirit and fire in Acts chapter two. They received both, the Holy Spirit and the fire. You must, I must, receive both if we want to be changed. Many people receive the Holy Spirit but never yield to the baptism of fire. The baptism of fire is what changes your tongue.

Without the third level of baptism, we can be saved and filled with the Holy Spirit and even speak in tongues more than others, but when we receive the third level of fire baptism our tongues sound like heaven. Our tongues speak love and life, not death and defeat! We become firetalkers and firewalkers.

James chapter three says that a human tongue cannot be tamed. James talked of the tongue and fire.

Even so the tongue is a little member, and it can boast of great things. See how much wood or how great a forest a tiny spark can set ablaze! And the tongue is a fire. [The tongue is a] world of wickedness set among our members, contaminating and depraving the whole body and setting on fire the wheel of birth (the cycle of man's nature), being itself ignited by hell (Gehenna). But the human tongue can be tamed by no man. It is a restless (undisciplined, irreconcilable) evil, full of deadly poison. With it we bless the Lord and Father, and with it we curse men who were made in God's likeness! Out of the same mouth come forth blessing and cursing. These things, my brethren ought not to be so. James 3:5-6, 8-10

After reading what James said about the human tongue it is much easier to understand why there must be a third baptism of fire.

God sets a spirit backfire to stop the natural tongue of fire that contaminates and depraves the whole body! God saves us from our own human fire tongue and gives us a God fire tongue! Listen to how you talk. Your tongue will tell you the level of your baptism. A fire talker is an eternal life talker at all times, no woe is me, no 'me' at all! A fire baptized tongue speaks life and life more abundantly; a fire baptized tongue speaks with power and authority.

When you receive the baptism of the Holy Spirit but you refuse the baptism of your tongue with fire, your language never changes. You still talk like the world, and you will sound like the world. God offers us through the third baptism an opportunity to sound like heaven instead of earth, but we must choose to accept the fire of God. We can either receive the baptism of fire and become purified, or we will receive the fire of God and be judged by it.

Let's go back to Acts and see what happened. One hundred and twenty people received the sound of heaven, and then a new fire tongue sat upon each one of their heads. When God's fire tongue gets on your head it changes the way you think. It changes the way you speak.

The most negative person in the world who seems to be able to only speak gloom and doom turns quickly and sounds like heaven! Your speech will change; your sound will change once you allow the fire of God's Holy Spirit to fully immerse you in this final fire baptism!

Once they all received the new fire tongue and it settled on each one of them, they were all filled with the Holy Spirit and began to speak differently! They spoke in foreign languages. They spoke languages that they didn't even mentally know! But there were many people hearing them!

That means they must have been loud! They were in an upper room, and people on the street below heard them speaking in their own languages. I have been filled with the Holy Spirit and received the third baptism of my tongue of fire for almost fifty years. Over those years I have had numerous people come up to me after a service and tell me I was singing, or speaking in their native tongue.

One time I was at the piano in a large church, and I was flowing in a song of the Holy Spirit in tongues and interpretation. Afterwards a man from Israel came up to me and said, "Thank you for singing in Hebrew today. It made me feel so at home in this house of worship." I simply thanked him, but I knew it was the Holy Spirit as I do not know the Hebrew language.

Recently we were ministering in an all-Spanish speaking church. No one there spoke English other than the female pastor who spoke both English and Spanish. I wanted to worship with them, so I chose one of my songs that we built a long open bridge in the track so I can sing in the spirit, and as the Holy Spirit gives me the interpretation, I can sing that also. When I started singing in the Holy Spirit language the people started cheering and shouting and lifting their hands! I was so excited and said to myself, "They sure do love the Holy Spirit here." I kept singing in the Spirit, and they kept cheering.

Afterwards we went to lunch with the pastors, and I commented to them how much their people love the Holy Spirit when He moves. She started laughing and said, "Yes, they do love the Holy Spirit. But you were singing in fluent Spanish, and that blessed them so much. They thought that you were fluent in our language so they cheered." I started laughing and said that I can barely speak English, and it is so mixed with my southern and country drawls! We had a good laugh that day, but I loved how Holy Spirit will do what He wants to do, when He wants to do it, if we will only stay yielded to Him.

We must stay saturated in the oil of the Holy Spirit and the fire of the Spirit of God to remain ready at all times for His coming and His use. Don't be surprised when you walk in all three levels of baptism that people just don't 'get you.' God calls you a peculiar people. Own it! Enjoy it. You are different on purpose!

In Acts chapter two the people hearing the one hundred and twenty freshly baptized in the Holy Spirit and fire were astonished, and bewildered, and amazed at them. They also accused them of being drunk! I believe the reason they thought they were drunk is not because they were stumbling around, but because they were so bold and full of authority and power. They were so assured and had no insecurity at all!

When you have been baptized in water, the Holy Spirit, and fire you have the power and authority of God inside of you at all times. Death and life are in the power of your tongue at all times. The devil is afraid of you when your tongue is baptized with heaven's fire. Everywhere you go and everything you say starts fires around you! Before you know it, you are like the three Hebrew children in Daniel chapter three! You walk in the midst of the fire with God! You are a firewalker, firetalker, and firestarter!

When this happens you are finally doing and being what you were created to do and be. You have taken fallen Lucifer's place as you walk in the midst of God's presence, up and down in the midst of the stones of fire you worship holy Father God! You have successfully taken your place as a worshiper on fire for God's glory. Welcome to the fire family!

Chapter Twelve
The Holy Spirit Speaks and Sings through You

Therefore, the person who speaks in an [unknown] tongue should pray [for the power] to interpret and explain what he says. For if I pray in an [unknown] tongue, my spirit [by the Holy Spirit within me] prays, but my mind is unproductive [it bears no fruit and helps nobody]. Then what am I to do? I will pray with my spirit [by the Holy Spirit that is within me], but I will also pray [intelligently] with my mind and understanding; I will sing with my spirit [by the Holy Spirit that is within me], but I will sing [intelligently] with my mind and understanding also. 1 Corinthians 14:13-15

I have been teaching our School Of Worship sessions for many years. On the very first day everyone who hasn't already been filled with the Holy Spirit gets filled with the Holy Spirit. By the end of the first day everyone can sing in their Holy Spirit language. The first thing everyone must learn is that Holy Spirit wants to sing through you in tongues! All I have to do is show everyone the verses above and the proof is right there.

As far as we know Paul was not a musician or even a singer, but once you are truly filled with the Holy Spirit and have yielded your vocal instrument to the control of Holy Spirit, He wants to sing! Holy Spirit wants to worship Father through your instrument! (Romans 6:13)

As we learn that yielding has nothing to do with what we call 'talent' but rather we are an instrument in God's orchestra, and He wants to hear us! He loves our sound, especially once our sound is yielded to Holy Spirit, and we sound like heaven!

The second day everyone is always so happy and excited for circle time because they have already sung in their Holy Spirit language in front of everybody, and they are ready to do it again! The second day we learn how to interpret! You should see the faces of those who just one day prior were hoping and praying that I would not ask them to sing in tongues. On the second day they are hoping and fervently praying that I will ask them to sing in tongues and not sing in the interpretation! By the end of the second day everyone is singing in both tongues and interpretation.

Why is this so important to me that everyone learn to yield to Holy Spirit and manifest the eighth and ninth gifts? It is so important to me because it was so important to the Spirit of God when the Bible was written, and it made the cut on the edit table. The verses in 1 Corinthians are in the Bible to help us learn how to yield to Holy Spirit with our voices and get over ourselves, our insecurities, our self-focus, and our pride! Once we learn to use our 'tongue of fire' from heaven, instead of our fiery tongue from earth, our lives can begin to be fruit filled of Holy Spirit, and all nine of His gifts can manifest in our lives as He wills it.

One of the studies I use when helping people learn how to yield to the baptism of the Holy Spirit and to yield their tongues to the baptism of fire is from a University of Pennsylvania Medical School paper written on speaking in tongues.

The article was published in the Penn Medicine News on October 30, 2006. The title of the article is: Language Center of the Brain is Not Under the Control of Subjects Who "Speak in Tongues." The subtitle is, "First Neuroimaging Examination of Participants Practicing Glossolalia Shows Decreased Cerebral Activity," Penn Study Shows. When I first saw this article, I was so excited to read it, then I read it, and I have been sharing it ever since!

You can look up the full article with the information above but let me share portions of what was written.

"Researchers at the University of Pennsylvania School Of Medicine have discovered decreased activity in the frontal lobes, an area of the brain associated with being in control of one's self.

This pioneering study, involving functional imaging of the brain while subjects were speaking in tongues, is in the November issue Psychiatry Research: Neuroimaging, the official publication of the International Society for Neuroimaging in Psychiatry.

Radiology investigators observed increased or decreased brain activity - by measuring regional cerebral blood flow with SPECT (Single Photon Emission Computed Tomography) imaging - while the subjects were speaking in tongues. They then compared the imaging to what happened to the brain while the subjects sang gospel music.

"We noticed a number of changes that occurred functionally in the brain," comments Principal Investigator Andrew

Newberg, MD, Associate Professor of Radiology, Psychiatry, and Religious Studies, and Director for the Center of Spirituality and the Mind, at Penn. "Our finding of decreased activity in the frontal lobes during the practice of speaking in tongues is fascinating because these subjects truly believe that the Spirit of God is moving through them and controlling them to speak. Our brain imaging research shows us that these subjects are not in control of the usual language centers during this activity, which is consistent with their description of a lack of intentional control while speaking in tongues."

He went on to say a little further in the article that, "This study also showed a number of other changes in the brain, including those areas involved in emotions and establishing our sense of self."

If you would like to look up this article to read, you can find it at http://www.uphs.upenn.edue/news/News_Releases/oct06/glossolalia.htm

The world is paying attention to the power of the Holy Spirit while speaking in tongues! Did you notice that one of his findings lines up perfectly with the Word of God and our self-worth?

He who speaks in a [strange] tongue edifies and improves himself . . . 1 Corinthians 14:4

The Bible tells us when we pray in the language of heaven, when Holy Spirit prays through us, or speaks through us that we are personally edified and improved! The scientists in the above article proved the exact same thing while observing the brain during the time a person was speaking in tongues.

If you feel bad about yourself, or you are fighting insecurities, fear, depression, anxiety, etc. pray in tongues! Let the Holy

Spirit pray through you. The yielding of oneself to the Spirit of God edifies and improves you!

Can you imagine? The best self-help tool in the universe is praying in tongues! It edifies and improves you! Who doesn't need edifying and improving? I know I do! Let's stop for a moment and pray in tongues!

Paul taught extensively on praying in tongues and the benefits of it. He also said, and I quoted him in the very first scriptures of this chapter, that he himself prayed in tongues and interpreted, and he sang in tongues and interpreted. Paul expounded on several manifested gifts of the Holy Spirit in chapter fourteen. He focused mainly on tongues, interpretation, and prophesy because these gifts can bring great edification to the whole body of Christ when in operation in organized services.

You may not have noticed, but look around and you will see. The whole body of Christ is in great need of edification and improvement! We can allow Holy Spirit to pray and sing through us, then we yield to the same Holy Spirit to interpret and prophesy through us. When we are fully yielded and our tongues have been baptized in fire speaking the sounds of heaven and not the people pleasing sounds of earth, the body of Christ will rise higher and higher!

It is the same Holy Spirit that uses us for all His gifts to manifest through us for the benefit of others. We don't pick and choose which gifts we want to manifest. It is His will flowing through our yielded instruments that bring about the working of the sounds of heaven in an organized service. We are the instruments! We no longer have a will. We have yielded our wills to the will of the Holy Spirit.

Once I have been baptized in all three levels of service; water,

Holy Spirit, and fire, then I don't have the right to say to Father God, "I don't feel like it today." We gave up that right when we yielded ourselves to His will.

Jesus yielded Himself to that level in the Garden of Gethsemane.

Father, if You are willing, remove this cup from Me; yet not My will, but [always] Yours be done. Luke 22:42

We want to follow Jesus? Then we must yield to the same level that He did. Ask yourself this question. What are you willing to do to follow Christ? Your answer confirms your destiny.

Chapter Thirteen
The Hierarchy of the Kingdom of God

A few years ago we were preparing for a mini-School of Worship for a church in Fontana, CA, Church of the Hand of God. As I was praying in the Holy Spirit and drying my hair, I had a vision. Visions come quickly, like a flash of lightning for me. I see in an instant of heaven time, what could take me weeks to share with words in earth time.

In this particular vision I first saw a heading, and heard it read to me. The heading was THE HIERARCHY OF THE KINGDOM OF GOD. It was in all caps, and I heard it read like an announcement being given to me.

First of all, I don't even use that word, 'hierarchy.' It's not in my vocabulary. That's one of the ways I know when I hear from heaven. The Holy Spirit tends to use words that I am unfamiliar with, or don't regularly use when speaking.

I will endeavor to share this massive in-depth vision in as few words as possible, but I can make no guarantees. Visions from heaven are not just linear. They are vertical, horizontal, and spherical all at the same time. If you could imagine a huge round ball of light and in every degree of direction there was an infinity arrow exploding out of the ball. That's what a vision from heaven is for me.

I will spend all of eternity slowing down the visions enough to speak of them. I will share in this chapter as much information that I have been able to assimilate to earth words.

Let's begin with the definition of the word hierarchy. I had to look it up in the dictionary. As a noun it means a system or organization in which people or groups are ranked one above the other according to status or authority. Its origin is late Middle English: via Old French and medieval Latin from Greek hierarkhia, from hierarkhes 'sacred ruler.' The earliest sense was 'system of orders of angels and heavenly beings;' the other senses date from the 17th century.

Ok, enough of what the dictionary says. That's enough to let you know what I first saw. I saw order, God's order, rank, and file. I saw a vertical picture of the levels of power and authority set in place by our Father God.

I knew instinctively that the Holy Spirit was allowing me to see this so I could teach it, share it, and give it to others. I also knew Holy Spirit was showing me my own position in the Hierarchy of the Kingdom of God.

Even though this and all visions I have had happen in a flash, an instant, a moment in earth time, it is as if earth time goes into slow motion while God calls me upward into a time and space that is moving in His time. I saw the big heading, or banner then I saw the alignment of levels of authority and power. I will do my best to show you.

HIERARCHY OF THE KINGDOM OF GOD

GOD	GOD	GOD
SON JESUS	FATHER	HOLY SPIRIT
Father's Image & Authority	Massive	Shekinah = Feminine
Word and Power	Infinite Dimension	Glory Expression of God
		Spirit & Power
		GLORY (light)
		HONOR (open door)
		1 Corinthians 12 - 9 gifts

Three corresponding archangels - kingdom authority assumed

Michael	Gabriel	Lucifer
Warrior	Word	Worship

Nine stones
He fell (Ex.28, Is. 14, Rev.21)
Lost his position
God made mankind to replace him
Man made a little lower than God
(Ps. 8:5 crowned in glory and honor)
Heb. 2: 7-9 (AMP)
Romans 6:13 (instruments in us –
our tones, DNA cellular levels)
1 Cor. 6:19 – Our body
houses the Holy Ghost
Mankind took Lucifer's place
under the authority of the Holy Spirit

Man was made a little lower than God to house the dominion and carry the authority of

ALL 3 ARCHANGELS

WARRIOR	WORD	WORSHIP
	MALE	FEMALE

Agreement brings
GOD

Once we yield to the Holy Spirit and accept His presence fully we immediately take Lucifer's position as archangel of worship. Lucifer was under the direction of the Godhead Holy Spirit. I believe that is why the only scripture in the entire Bible that can cause a person to lose their position in God's kingdom is to blaspheme the Holy Spirit. That is what Lucifer did! He stopped yielding to His Godhead covering. He rebelled against the Holy Spirit, and Father threw him out of heaven forever because of it.

And everyone who makes a statement or speaks a word against the Son of Man, it will be forgiven him; but he who blasphemes against the Holy Spirit [that is, whoever intentionally comes short of the reverence due the Holy Spirit], it will not be forgiven him [for him there is no forgiveness]. Luke 12:10

Do not quench (suppress or subdue) the [Holy] Spirit.
1 Thessalonians 5:19

Father God takes very seriously our response to His gift of the Holy Spirit. Jesus told the disciples that Father would send His replacement, His representative, the Holy Spirit. If we accept Father's gift of Holy Spirit we are immediately taking our position in the archangel level of authority in the hierarchy of the kingdom of God. We step up in our rank and order simply by our yielding to Holy Spirit.

I don't think I have to point out that Holy Spirit has nine different fruit and nine different manifested gifts. Notice and recognize that Lucifer before he fell had nine different covering stones. Once he fell those fiery stones were stripped from his covering. He lost his Holy Spirit fire; he lost his light bearing stones. He lost his pure and holy sound. He lost everything.

God sealed the entire fall and made it plain in the Bible that messing with the Holy Spirit would not be tolerated. He had already proven what would happen as he threw Satan out of heaven, out of his hierarchy position of rank and order.

Jesus said that He witnessed the fall of Satan.

I saw Satan falling like lightning [flash] from heaven. Behold! I have given you authority and power to trample upon serpents and scorpions, and [physical and mental strength and ability] over all the power that the enemy [possesses]; and nothing shall in any way harm you. Luke 10:18-19

Once Satan was thrown out of heaven he lost all ability, authority, and power over you. Jesus said that He gave us authority and power to trample all over the devil and his demons, and nothing will harm us when we are in our proper position of rank and authority in the hierarchy of the kingdom of God.

A few years ago, Father showed me this vision while I was praying in the Holy Spirit. You want to know more? You want to see more? Pray in the Holy Spirit. Yield to the Holy Spirit. Allow full access to your instrument, and take your position under the control of the Holy Spirit!

Not everyone who says, 'Lord, Lord' will enter the kingdom of heaven.

Not everyone who says to Me, Lord, Lord, will enter the kingdom of heaven, but he who does the will of My Father Who is in heaven. Matthew 7:21

Jesus said there will be those who call Him Lord, but they won't enter the kingdom of heaven. It takes more than just mental assent to who Jesus is. It takes more than water baptism to enter the kingdom of heaven and take your rightful

God given position. Every gift Father gives is good.

Every good gift and every perfect (free, large, full) gift is from above; it comes down from the Father of all [that gives] light, in [the shining of] Whom there can be no variation [rising or setting] or shadow cast by His turning [as in an eclipse]. James 1:17

If you then, evil as you are, know how to give good gifts [gifts that are to their advantage] to your children, how much more will your heavenly Father give the Holy Spirit to those who ask and continue to ask Him! Luke 11:13

The Holy Spirit is Father God's gift to those of us who will ask Him. If we don't ask, how can we receive? If we don't receive the Holy Spirit then we can't take our rightful position in the hierarchy of the kingdom of heaven. Get into position my friend. You were called and created for such a time as this!

Because of what Jesus did for us, not only can we step into the archangel position of worship, taking Lucifer's fallen position, but we can also stand beside Michael, the archangel of war under the authority of King Jesus, our Prince of Peace. The word prince is actually translated warrior in the ancient Hebrew. King Jesus is our Warrior Prince of Peace!

We don't take Michael's position because he didn't lose it! We step up alongside Michael and war with him, under the authority of his Godhead covering, King Jesus! That is why in Revelation chapter twenty-one the bride of Christ is revealed as having all nine stones that Lucifer lost in his fall, plus three more new stones for Christ's bride! Three is the number for the bride, and with all of fallen Lucifer's stones covering Christ's bride she is easily identified.

Christ's bride has these nine fiery stones because she has

accepted all three levels of baptism: water, Holy Spirit, and fire. She has everything Lucifer lost in his fall from his rank and position in the hierarchy of the kingdom of heaven. She stands alongside her Warrior Prince King Jesus and battles the antichrist, beast and false prophet in the last war to be fought! She not only has the right to be there, she has the authority to be there!

Behold, I am going to come like a thief! Blessed (happy, to be envied) is he who stays awake (alert) and who guards his clothes, so that he may not be naked and [have the shame of being] seen exposed! And they gathered them together at the place which in Hebrew is called Armageddon.
Revelation 16:15-16

The bride will be covered in her fiery stones of worship, and she will have her armor covering of Jesus' righteousness. She will have one more position as she stands in full authority also. Gabriel is the archangel of the Word of God under the authority of Father God. We who have filled our mouths with His word while here on earth, can take our position beside Gabriel in rank and authority of the Word of God!

We cannot allow traditions or even our religious backgrounds to get in the way of God's rank and authority for us. By not receiving the power of God's gift through the Holy Spirit to us we sometimes can't discern the difference between the soul and the spirit.

Thus you are nullifying and making void and of no effect [the authority of] the Word of God through your tradition, which you [in turn] hand on. And many things of this kind you are doing. Mark 7:13

Behold! I have given you authority and power to trample upon serpents and scorpions, and [physical and mental strength and ability] over all the power that the enemy [possesses]; and nothing shall in any way harm you. Luke 10:19

Jesus was speaking plainly to His followers that once Lucifer fell and lost his position that we were given access to the rank of archangel in the hierarchy of the kingdom of God. Let me close this chapter with my favorite verses of authority given to us through Jesus Christ, God's holy Word, and the Holy Spirit.

In conclusion, be strong in the Lord [be empowered through your union with Him]; draw your strength from Him [that strength which His boundless might provides]. Put on God's whole armor [the armor of a heavy-armed soldier which God supplies], that you may be able successfully to stand up against [all] the strategies and the deceits of the devil. For we are not wrestling with flesh and blood [contending only with physical opponents], but against the despotisms, against the powers, against [the master spirits who are] the world rulers of this present darkness, against the spirit forces of wickedness in the heavenly (supernatural) sphere. Therefore put on God's complete armor, that you may be able to resist and stand your ground on the evil day [of danger], and, having done all [the crisis demands], to stand [firmly in your place]. Stand therefore [hold your ground], having tightened the belt of truth around your loins and having put on the breastplate of integrity and of moral rectitude and right standing with God, and having shod your feet in preparation [to face the enemy with the firm-footed stability, the promptness, and the readiness produced by the good news] of the Gospel of peace. Lift up over all the [covering] shield of saving faith, upon which you can quench all the flaming missiles of the wicked [one]. And take the helmet of salvation and the sword that the Spirit wields, which is the Word of God. Pray at all times (on every occasion, in every season) in the Spirit, with all [manner of] prayer and entreaty. To that end keep alert and watch with strong purpose and perseverance, interceding in behalf of all the saints (God's consecrated people). Ephesians 6:10-18

With all of that scripture I could spend a year and thousands of pages teaching on spiritual warfare. I will save that for my next book, Pray, Warrior, Pray!

Notice in verse 17 that the sword that the Spirit within us wields is the Word of God. If you don't fill yourself up with the Word of God then the Holy Spirit within you has no sword to wield on your behalf! Don't have secondhand knowledge of the Word of God. Get in the Word and stay in the Word the rest of your life, and take your position alongside Gabriel as Warrior Word Worshiper! Warrior Word Worshiper is available to you as your rank and authority in the hierarchy of the kingdom of God, but only you can submit to the three levels of baptism that create the submitted levels of your spirit, soul, and body.

Three levels of baptism create the path for your position of three levels of archangel authority just a little lower than God. We must always stay submitted to the triune Godhead. King Jesus is our Warrior Prince of Peace. He is Commander and Chief. He gives the orders; we obey them. Father God reveals Himself and His orders to us through His Word. Without His Word we can never know Father. Jesus is the way to the Father. Jesus is the Word made flesh. There is only one way to heaven; there is only one way back to Father, it is in order of rank and authority.

Accept Jesus, fill your life with His Word, and be filled with Holy Spirit. Yield your entire being to Holy Spirit. Don't disobey, quench, resist, or blaspheme the Holy Spirit.

Too many people think that in heaven they will be this or that. Too many people think that on the way up to heaven they will be changed into something or someone else. But the truth is the earth is the womb of heaven. We must develop here into who we will be for eternity. Whatever rank you leave this earth will be the rank you enter the kingdom of heaven.

He who is unrighteous (unjust, wicked), let him be unrighteous still; and he who is filthy (vile, impure), let him be filthy still; and he who is righteous (just, upright, in right standing with God), let him do right still; and he who is holy, let him be holy still. Revelation 22:11

Whoever you develop into on earth is how you will enter heaven. There will be no do-overs once you get there. Don't waste your time here being earthly and sounding like the earth. Yield beloved. Yield to Son, Father, and Holy Spirit. Take your position!

Chapter Fourteen
How to be Led by Holy Spirit

But I say, walk and live [habitually] in the [Holy] Spirit [responsive to and controlled and guided by the Spirit]; then you will certainly not gratify the cravings and desires of the flesh (of human nature without God). For the desires of the flesh are opposed to the [Holy] Spirit, and the [desires of the] Spirit are opposed to the flesh (godless human nature); for these are antagonistic to each other [continually withstanding and in conflict with each other], so that you are not free but are prevented from doing what you desire to do. But if you are guided (led) by the [Holy] Spirit, you are not subject to the Law. Galatians 5:16-18

Being led by the Holy Spirit takes a constant act of submission on our parts. Submission to the Holy Spirit is to willingly go under the mission of Holy Spirit. Even when I want to go another way, submission means I choose to override my own desires and go the way of the Holy Spirit.

For all who are led by the Spirit of God are sons of God. Romans 8:14

I want to be a child of God. I want to be counted in the family and not just be a servant of God, but His very own child. To be His child means to be led by His Spirit and only His Spirit. This is an act of my own will to choose to submit, to go under, to stay under, and not stick my own head up in the air with my own idea. This takes a lifetime commitment. It takes regularly starting over because of failure to submit yesterday, or the day before, or whenever or wherever my own will gets in the way of the Holy Spirit leading me.

You will fail sometimes. We have an Advocate with the Father through Jesus Christ, and the Holy Spirit. Both advocate for us in the court of heaven when we need help. And I need help regularly!

If we [freely] admit that we have sinned and confess our sins, He is faithful and just (true to His own nature and promises) and will forgive our sins [dismiss our lawlessness] and [continuously] cleanse us from all unrighteousness [everything not in conformity to His will in purpose, thought, and action]. 1 John 1:9

My little children, I write you these things so that you may not violate God's law and sin. But if anyone should sin, we have an Advocate (One Who will intercede for us) with the Father - [it is] Jesus Christ [the all] righteous [upright, just, Who conforms to the Father's will in every purpose, thought, and action]. 1 John 2:1

Jesus called the Holy Spirit our Advocate also.

And I will ask the Father, and He will give you another Comforter (Counselor, Helper, Intercessor, Advocate, Strengthener, and Standby), that He may remain with you forever. John 14:16

But when the Comforter (Counselor, Helper, Advocate, Intercessor, Strengthener, Standby) comes, Whom I will send to you from the Father, the Spirit of Truth Who comes (proceeds) from the Father, He [Himself] will testify regarding Me. John 15:26

Jesus taught His disciples how to be led by the Holy Spirit as He kept showing them, and telling them Who Holy Spirit was. He was teaching them to know Holy Spirit so they would trust Him to lead them daily.

We see how Father expects us to be bearing the fruit of the Holy Spirit in abundance.

When you bear (produce) much fruit, My Father is honored and glorified, and you show and prove yourselves to be true followers of Mine. John 15:8

To be led by Holy Spirit causes us to have to be filled with His fruit. If I have to have my own way then I am not walking in love, joy, peace, nor patience. The whole Book of 1 John gives detailed explanations about the love of God flowing through us showing that we are truly His children. This particular Book of 1 John talks at length about loving one another, and if we don't love one another then we are not His children. But the best verse to tie it all up neatly in a bow as Father, Son, and Holy Spirit led is the final verse.

All who keep His commandments [who obey His orders and follow His plan, live and continue to live, to stay and] abide in Him, and He in them. [They let Christ be a home to them and they are the home of Christ.] And by this we know and understand and have the proof that He [really] lives and makes His home in us: by the [Holy] Spirit Whom He has given us. 1 John 3:24

Many people say they love the Lord God. Many people say that Jesus lives in their hearts. But the scripture above shows us the final proof of these two statements. By this we know and understand and have the proof. He really lives and makes His home in us when the Holy Spirit is manifesting Who He is from within us! To be called sons of God means we are led by the Holy Spirit at all times. We love when others don't. We forgive when others can't. We are filled with joy and peace when everyone else seems to be losing their minds. We exude kindness and goodness toward others when most people are so selfish and self-focused.

Most people have lost their ability to be loyal or faithful in this generation. But when we are filled with the Holy Spirit we walk by faith and not by sight. To be led by the Holy Spirit means we are not afraid when others have shrunk back in fear.

How are we led by the Holy Spirit? That is completely up to you and your choice to allow Him to lead. He will always take the lead when you give it up. He won't make you move over and let Him drive. He won't make you stop, so He can start. You are fully in control of being led by the Holy Spirit.

When you decide to let Him lead, He knows when you really mean it, and you have conquered all your tormenting demons of needing to be in control and having to be in charge. He won't fight you for the lead. If you want to lead, He will let you. If you go the wrong way, and you will when you are leading, He will let you.

You don't know the way, and you can't see what's ahead, but He knows the way, He sees what is ahead and in truth, He has already been there with you in your future. So it all comes down to how long will you wrestle with the Spirit of God for the lead?

When our daughter went to heaven there were no answers to help heal our broken hearts. There were no great revelations that brought closure to why a six-year-old precious worshiper developed an inoperable brain tumor and died in less than a year. There was nothing to soothe our shattered lives.

One morning as I poured myself out (every morning) at His feet, searching for something, anything to help me move forward for one more day, I was crying out and weeping before the Lord, and I heard Holy Spirit say, "Do you trust Me?" I had just been reading that story of the conversation between Jesus and Peter in John twenty-one. Jesus kept asking Peter, Do you love Me? Peter became frustrated because he knew Jesus was questioning his love for Him. I had that story in my mind when the Holy Spirit said, "Do you trust Me?"

I was honest with the Lord and said, "I want to trust You." He knew my heart and He knew that I was struggling to trust Him after Gabrielle died. I never, for one moment, thought she would die. I believed, we all believed, that she would live, so much so that we didn't even embalm her body, and her brothers put a 'jiggle doll' in the casket with her to make noise when she rose from the dead. We believed. It was months after she had gone to heaven, and somehow, I can't explain it, but I still believed. That's when the Holy Spirit told me, "Gabrielle is not in your past, but she is in your future."

I knew from that moment on, that she was truly alive and well and living ahead of me. From that revelation forward I could truly say, "Yes, Lord. I trust You." These times of brokenness can either make us or break us. This one made me. I have been fully submitted to the leading of the Holy Spirit since that moment, and I am a daughter of the King. He's my Father, and I am His daughter.

So, come out from among [unbelievers], and separate (sever) yourselves from them, says the Lord, and touch not [any] unclean thing; then I will receive you kindly and treat you with favor, and I will be a Father to you, and you shall be My sons and daughters, says the Lord Almighty. 2 Corinthians 6:17-18

To be led by the Holy Spirit means you cannot belong to another. He is a jealous God, an all-consuming fire. Receive all of Him, Father, His Son, and His Holy Spirit. Then you will be His family, and He will be yours.

It all comes down to trust. Most people have some level of trust issues, and this is one of those personal stumbling blocks that must be dealt with to be fully led by the Holy Spirit. How do I trust the Holy Spirit? You decide to do just that, and then you do it. It may last a whole hour the first time you decide to trust Him. Then you start all over again and make the second decision to trust Him.

This may go on and on for many days, weeks, months and with some people even years. But as long as you keep deciding and follow through with your action, He will keep leading you. Even when you fail and miss it and take the reins back over and over again, He still trusts you to do the right thing and let Him lead you.

That's who He is. When we are completely not trustworthy, He trusts us to make the right decision and let Him lead. When Holy Spirit is completely trustworthy, we withhold our trust from Him. If you have tried a thousand times to trust Him and let Him lead you, then try it one thousand and one. He can take all your insecurities, broken places, and mixed-up emotions. In fact, the only way you are ever going to get past your past situations, circumstances, and compromised relationships is to trust Him. While you let Him lead you, He will also begin to heal you, and train you, and help you, and sustain you. That is who He is.

Let Him lead. You will always be going the right way when Holy Spirit is navigating the journey. He takes no side roads, nor does He ever get lost. He has already been there with you in your future, so He knows the way.

Let Him lead; you will thank me one day.

Chapter Fifteen
The Seven-Fold Spirits of God

And to the angel (messenger) of the assembly (church) in Sardis write: These are the words of Him Who has the seven Spirits of God [the sevenfold Holy Spirit] and the seven stars . . . Revelation 3:1

Out from the throne came flashes of lightning and rumblings and peals of thunder, and in front of the throne seven blazing torches burned, which are the seven Spirits of God [the sevenfold Holy Spirit] . . . Revelation 4:5

And there between the throne and the four living creatures (beings) and among the elders [of the heavenly Sanhedrin] I saw a Lamb standing, as though it had been slain, with seven horns and with seven eyes, which are the seven Spirits of God [the sevenfold Holy Spirit] Who have been sent [on duty far and wide] into all the earth. Revelation 5:6

There are three verses that reveal the Holy Spirit as the sevenfold Spirits of God. From the first passage we see that the Holy Spirit has words and He speaks. In the second passage of scripture, we see that the Holy Spirit is seven blazing torches on fire! In the third passage we see that the sevenfold Holy Spirit has been sent into all the earth and is on duty far and wide.

The way Holy Spirit speaks is through you and me and people like us who are willing to be led by, yielded to, and filled with the Holy Spirit. We manifest Who He is in every way that He wants to manifest. Holy Spirit is on duty all over the earth!

The most specific of all the scripture passages on the sevenfold Holy Spirit is in Isaiah.

And there shall come forth a Shoot out of the stock of Jesse [David's father], and a Branch out of his roots shall grow and bear fruit. And the Spirit of the Lord shall rest upon Him-the Spirit of wisdom and understanding, the Spirit of counsel and might, the Spirit of knowledge and of reverential and obedient fear of the Lord . . . Isaiah 11:1-2

Notice that this is a prophetic passage about the coming Messiah, Jesus Christ. He will come forth through Jesse, and David. He will be a Branch and will grow and bear fruit. His fruit will be the fruit of the sevenfold Holy Spirit. If we list what we see above we can easily see six manifested Spirits of Holy Spirit.

1. Spirit of wisdom
2. Spirit of understanding
3. Spirit of counsel
4. Spirit of might
5. Spirit of knowledge
6. Spirit of reverential and obedient fear of the Lord

So where is the seventh of the sevenfold Spirits of God? It is not the seventh Spirit we are missing. It is the first.

1. Spirit of holy
2. Spirit of wisdom
3. Spirit of understanding
4. Spirit of counsel
5. Spirit of might
6. Spirit of knowledge
7. Spirit of the fear of the Lord

Without the Spirit of holy there are no other manifestations of the sevenfold Spirits of God. He starts with holy. We must start with holy, set apart lives to be used by Holy Spirit. He fills our bodies, our temples, and makes us holy because He is holy. Too many times we try and manifest one of the gifts of the Holy Spirit simply because we long to be noticed, to be seen, to be recognized. All of this is rooted in pride and must go before He will manifest through us.

The sevenfold Spirits of God begin with holy and end with the fear of the Lord. Everything else is housed between these two Spirits. Much like the Ark of the Covenant that was covered with two massive angel beings with their wings spread out, we house the very presence of the Lord within our bodies, and we are covered with the sevenfold Spirits of God. The Spirits of holy and fear of the Lord cover us at all times, creating within us the ability to release any and all of His manifested gifts to benefit others. These gifts only manifest at His will, not ours. These gifts only manifest to benefit others, not to puff us up in pride. Holy Spirit will not manifest through us, 'proud as a peacock' strutting around.

After all these chapters we have built a container within you that is holy, filled with wisdom, understanding, counsel, might, knowledge and the fear of the Lord. Without the Spirit of holy, you won't survive His presence. Without the Spirit of the fear the Lord, you won't survive your own flesh.

We must have all of Him within us, just like Jesus did. To be one with Father and Jesus we must have the third of the triune Godhead living inside of us. Jesus' prayer gives us the best picture possible of the triune will for us.

That they all may be one, [just] as You, Father, are in Me and I in You, that they also may be one in Us, so that the world may believe and be convinced that You have sent Me. I have given to them the glory and honor which You have given Me, that they may be one [even] as We are one: I in them and You in Me, in order that they may become one and perfectly united, that the world may know and [definitely] recognize that You sent Me and that You have loved them [even] as You have loved Me. John 17:21-23

As Jesus was praying for His disciples, we can easily see how Holy Spirit creates a bridge, a union, between heaven, where Father God is, and earth, where Jesus is at the time of this prayer. Once Jesus received the Holy Spirit after John the Baptist, water baptized Him, He was filled with the sevenfold Spirits of God, the Holy Spirit.

The infilling of the Holy Spirit within Jesus, caused Him to graduate from being the Son of Man, to becoming one with Father God. The anointing on Him and in Him, created His destiny and purpose to be revealed. From that point on, Jesus was anointed, Jesus the Christ. From that point on, He was filled with and controlled by Holy Spirit, and His union with Father God was complete. Father God announced His graduation with these words, *This is My Son, My beloved, in Whom I delight.* Matthew 3:17

Jesus Christ was now walking in His full manifested and destined purpose on the earth. He was fully the Son of Man, and fully the Son of God. Union had been made through the infilling of the Holy Spirit. Jesus was one with Father through the Holy Spirit.

To fulfill our purpose and manifest our ordained calling and destiny we must accept our mission. We must accept fully the infilling of the sevenfold Spirits of God in the Holy Spirit and be united with Father through the Son and the Holy Spirit. Father first sent His only begotten Son, then He sent Holy Spirit both as our gifts from Him. Unless we choose to receive our gifts, we can never truly have them.

You may be given a gift from a friend. They may tell you they bought you a gift, 'and the next time we are together, I will give it to you,' they may say. But until you get the gift in your hand, and you open it up, unwrap it, and receive it as your own it's not yours.

Father sent Jesus as our gift. Unless we receive that gift, He is not ours. Jesus prayed for Father to send the gift of the Holy Spirit for us. Unless we receive this gift of the triune Godhead, we don't actually have Him. The gift given is not enough. The gift received is the true answer to all your problems on this earth, I truly believe.

Receiving the Holy Spirit won't magically make all your circumstances align, or your situations to rectify, or your natural relationships to all smooth out. That's not what I am saying. I am saying for the first time in your life when the storms come, you will have the right way through them. When the battles rage against you, a warrior will arise within you that knows how to win! You shall receive power when the Holy Spirit comes upon you! That was Jesus' final promise to His followers, and Father fulfilled it.

And behold, I will send forth upon you what My Father has

promised; but remain in the city [Jerusalem] until you are clothed with power from on high. Luke 24:49

Once you decide to house the sevenfold Spirits of God, the Holy Spirit, you will be clothed with power! Accept the very power of God to live inside you! The best part is you don't have to go to your closet each day and decide which of the seven jackets you would like to wear today. There is a covering cloak in you and on you that has been woven together for you called holy, wisdom, understanding, counsel, might, knowledge, and the fear of the Lord. Jesus wore it. Now you can too.

Chapter Sixteen
Holy Spirit is our Witness in Heaven and Earth

I am speaking the truth in Christ. I am not lying; my conscience [enlightened and prompted] by the Holy Spirit bearing witness with me. Romans 9:1

This is He Who came by (with) water and blood [His baptism and His death], Jesus Christ (the Messiah)-not by (in) the water only, but by (in) the water and the blood. And it is the [Holy] Spirit Who bears witness, because the [Holy] Spirit is the Truth. So there are three witnesses in heaven: the Father, the Word and the Holy Spirit, and these three are One; and there are three witnesses on the earth: the Spirit, the water, and the blood; and these three agree [are in unison; their testimony coincides]. 1 John 5:6-8

And we are witnesses of these things, and the Holy Spirit is also, Whom God has bestowed on those who obey Him.
Acts 5:32

And also, the Holy Spirit adds His testimony to us [in

confirmation of this]. Hebrews 10:15

It is easy to see that not only is the Holy Spirit living within us to help us accomplish all that Father has designed within us to accomplish, but Holy Spirit is also reporting back to the throne room as a witness. Depending on our obedience or disobedience His witness testimony is either for us or against us.

There are three witnesses in heaven: the Father, the Word, which is Jesus, and the Holy Spirit. All three witness either for us or against us depending on what we choose and how we live our lives. There are three witnesses on the earth: the Holy Spirit, the water, which is the Word of God, and the blood of Jesus. Some would try and make the witness of water be one's choice to be water baptized. I would say that is a very religious viewpoint. It is much more likely that the water that witnesses for us or against us is the Word of God that we choose to live by and in each day.

So that He might sanctify her, having cleansed her by the washing of water with the Word . . . Ephesians 5:26

The blood as our witness is from Hebrews in the court of heaven's legal system.

And to Jesus, the Mediator (Go-between, Agent) of a new covenant, and the sprinkled blood which speaks [of mercy], a better and nobler and more gracious message than the blood of Abel [which cried out for vengeance]. Hebrews 12:24

As one of our precious witnesses Who witnesses for us out of mercy instead of vengeance, the blood of Jesus still cries out before the mercy seat of God. We have a divine Mediator, Go-between, and Agent, Jesus Christ, Whose blood negotiated for us a better covenant!

Glory to God! Thank You, my Lord, for witnessing for those who have chosen the blood. This is where we understand the pleading of the blood of Jesus. It is a legal term before the court of heaven, and the Righteous Judge. How do you plead? I plead the blood of Jesus as my only defense. The blood witnesses for me. The Holy Spirit witnesses for me. God's Word that washed and cleansed my life witnesses for me!

When we look at the Old Testament as Father God was talking about calling witnesses to His court, I found three references, and all three references said that He called heaven and earth to witness against us. Not once in the Old Testament could I find Father calling any witnesses for us.

I call heaven and earth to witness this day against you that I have set before you life and death, the blessings and the curses; therefore choose life, that you and your descendants may live . . . Deuteronomy 30:19

Gather to me all the elders of your tribes and your officers, that I may speak these words in their ears and call heaven and earth to witness against them. Deuteronomy 31:28

I call heaven and earth to witness against you this day that you shall soon utterly perish from the land which you are going over the Jordan to possess. You will not live long upon it but will be utterly destroyed. Deuteronomy 4:26

All three instances in Deuteronomy in the court of heaven were of God calling witnesses to witness against us. The devil, the accuser of the brethren, has always drug humanity into the court of heaven and used our own words against us. It doesn't take many moments for a person using their uncontrollable, untamable tongue, that James speaks of, to give the devil more than enough ammunition to win every court case against us.

I have watched enough cop shows on television to know the statement. You have the right to remain silent. Every word you say can and will be used against you. The cops weren't the first to do that. The devil started that and he uses every word you say against you in the court of heaven. You have the right to remain silent. Some of us need to exercise that right until we learn to receive the baptism of fire, and receive a new fire tongue instead of that untamable one that keeps you in trouble both on earth and in the court of heaven.

Once Jesus came to earth as our gift from Father God, and we received Him as our Lord and Savior, then we can move into our next level of sanctification, and receive the Holy Spirit to live within us. Finally, we receive the baptism of fire, which is our final yielding of every member of our body to Holy Spirit's fire. Now when we open our mouths Holy Spirit speaks through us, and we can be assured Holy Spirit will never say anything that the devil can use against us in the court of heaven!

Now that we are one through Jesus Christ, our Lord and Defense attorney, and Holy Spirit, our Co-Counsel with our defense, Father, Son, and Holy Spirit witness for us! Righteous Judge Himself bears witness for me! When the judge speaks on your behalf there is no higher word!

Instead of the Righteous Judge calling heaven and earth to witness against us, we have become one with Father, Son, and Holy Spirit. Now the Righteous Judge calls the Holy Spirit, the water of the Word of God, that has cleansed us from all unrighteousness (the Word became flesh and dwelt among us), and the blood of Jesus that cries out for mercy! All three witnesses now witness for us before the Righteous Judge! Our heavenly Defense team can't be beat!

We accept Jesus Christ, His Holy Spirit, and His fire. Now we are clean, sanctified, purified, and holy. We are filled and clothed with power from on high. We are fire walkers, fire talkers, and fire starters everywhere we go.

This is not a time to want to plead your own defense or be your own attorney. This is not the time to try and talk your way out of the choices you have made throughout your life. This is the right time to accept all that Jesus has done for you. This is the time, the right time, to receive Holy Spirit fully. This is the time to give up all human flesh control, and fully surrender to the Holy Spirit's fire. This is the time to pray, "Burn me up, Lord, on Your altar and leave nothing of me. Only You, do I want. I want nothing but You forever."

When Solomon had finished praying, the fire came down from heaven and consumed the burnt offering and the sacrifices, and the glory of the Lord filled the house. The priests could not enter the house of the Lord, because the glory of the Lord had filled the Lord's house. And when all the people of Israel saw how the fire came down and the glory of the Lord upon the house, they bowed with their faces upon the pavement and worshiped and praised the Lord, saying, For He is good, for His mercy and loving-kindness endure forever.
2 Chronicles 7:1-3

May we walk all the days of our lives so filled with Shekinah glory, God's Holy Spirit, that all the world may see Him. When Moses came down out of the presence of the Lord, his face shown so brightly with Shekinah glory, that he scared all the people of the nation. He had to wear a veil just to cover the glory. May we all be so filled with the Shekinah glory of the Lord that our faces shine, and the whole world can see Him, and know Him, through our obedience.

My prayer for you is that you will fully surrender to His will. Stop wrestling with His presence, and simply give in to His will for your life. It is so much more, so much better than you could ever imagine. You have had control a long time now, and look where it has gotten you. Why not let Him drive, let Him navigate, and you rest for the rest of your life filled with His glory, on fire for His purpose.

'Father, take not Your Holy Spirit from me,' was the constant prayer of one of my heroes of faith, Kathryn Kuhlman. I pray the same prayer now. Father, take not Your Holy Spirit from me, for I cannot live on this earth without Your Spirit within me.

I will close this book with a vision I recently had. It has been a very hard six months in both Harry's and my life. We both had the virus, Covid-19, and it was very hard. For eight days we fought side by side to live. This particular virus seems to be coded with the ability to look for any weakness in your body and specifically attacks your weaknesses. I have had colon cancer twice so along with all the other very difficult symptoms, severe headache, fever, chills, body aches, etc. I was attacked in my abdominal area. I could not stop vomiting. For eight days and nights I threw up constantly. I was severely dehydrated, and I could not keep food or water down. On the eighth day I felt my spirit begin to leave my body.

Harry was very sick too, and he must have seen it begin to happen because with what little strength he had he yelled at me. He called my name. I was suddenly back in my mind, and I grabbed my spirit and pulled it back into my body. From there I crawled to the bed and called our doctor. He prescribed other medications, and I began to get better. I had defeated death on the eighth day, and I was going to live.

The following day Harry took a turn for the worse, and his breathing was affected severely. I won't tell his story for it is not mine to tell, but I will tell you this. We fought hard to keep

Harry on the earth, and a week later, he had to go to the hospital. I could not produce enough oxygen to sustain him with the home machines that I had rented.

We battled every day for the following eleven days to keep Harry on the earth. The warrior in me rose up, and soon I will write a book on this spiritual warfare journey that I truly believe God has called us to learn how to fight His way in these last days before Jesus comes for His bride. Pray, Warrior, Pray was the voice from heaven within me night and day for the past six months.

In the midst of all this warfare one day I was fighting to stay positive and in faith. I asked the Lord to give me something. Show me something, Lord. I closed my eyes and began to pray in the Holy Spirit.

All of a sudden, my vision eyes were opened. All I could see was darkness. Darkness was covering the whole earth. I was seeing the whole earth, and it was totally covered in darkness. I asked the Holy Spirit to tell me where to look, and what to look for! Holy Spirit said, "Look to the horizon."

I looked as far as I could see, and there it was. I saw light coming up over the horizon! I saw it. It was barely there in the first moments, and then it began to grow. The light got brighter and more visible. The light was slowly rising on the horizon. I said to Holy Spirit, "I see it! I see the light on the horizon." Then I asked the Holy Spirit, "What is it? What is the light?" Holy Spirit began to tell me. "This is My glory. It is rising on the horizon. Prophesy to the light. Prophesy to My glory."

I began to say to the horizon, "Glory rise! Glory rise!" Then this song came out of me.

I can see the glory
Rising on horizon
I can see the glory
Rising higher and higher
Glory rise!
Glory rise!
Glory rise!

Father, send Your glory
To break the power of darkness
Father, send Your glory
Teach us how to triumph
Glory rise!
Glory rise!
Glory rise!

Rise higher and higher
Rise wider and wider
Rise higher and higher
Rise! Rise!

I can see the glory
Rising on horizon
I can see the glory
Rising higher and higher
Glory rise!
Glory rise!
Glory rise!

This became the song that I have sung these past few months, and as I sing, I am prophesying! I see light all around me now. There is no more darkness in my vision. Holy Spirit will teach us how to triumph, but we must yield, listen, and obey to walk in His glory. Obey Him. Do what He says, and you will triumph too.

The Bible uses many metaphors to describe Holy Spirit. Some seem to be opposite each other, like fire and water. These two extremes to describe Holy Spirit and His action within us show the vastness of the manifested presence of our living God through Holy Spirit. He is the fire that purifies us. He is the water that cleanses us. He is the gentle and calm presence of the dove upon us.

He brings about in each of our lives what we individually need to bring forth God's character and purpose within us. Father uses His very presence housed within our flesh to renovate our old man into His new and eternal being. Don't resist the Holy Spirit. Don't push and pull with His presence. Learn to follow His lead. Put your feet on His feet, and learn to dance at His tempo. He leads; we follow. Life eternal can begin today for all who will stop resisting His presence, and ask for a full emersion deep within Him. Holy Spirit come!

About the Author

Cheryl Salem walked the runway to become Miss America 1980, despite what appeared to be all odds stacked against her. A horrific car crash resulting in a physical handicap and over 100 stitches in her face, were no match for what God had planned for her life. Through childlike faith in Him, she overcame the obstacles and eventually took the crown in Atlantic City to become Miss America 1980. She has used this distinction as a springboard to launch the gospel into churches, women's conferences, and many television appearances. According to Cheryl, "None of these things would be possible, if not for my Jesus."

In 1985, Cheryl married the love of her life, Harry Salem II. Harry and Cheryl Salem travel the world ministering the gospel, telling people that Jesus loves them and that He is returning soon! Their lives revolve around seeking the Lord and where He would have them go. Two by two they travel, loving God's people, living and moving in His anointing.

In 1999, Harry and Cheryl endured the loss of their 6-year-old daughter, Gabrielle. As they boldly took steps of faith to overcome the agonizing pain of Gabrielle's death, they asked God to restore them and for souls to come into His kingdom. God has restored the Salem family and because of His mighty anointing, the altars have been full!

Harry and Cheryl are committed to leading godly lives as an example to their sons, Harry III and Roman. In 2012 Roman married a beautiful young lady, Stephanie, and she became their daughter-in-love. Healing and restoration came full circle to the Salem family with the miracle births of Roman and Stephanie's children, Mia Gabrielle and Roman Harry.

Cheryl and Harry have written over forty books. From her first book to her last, Cheryl's books are open and honest with such transparency you can almost hear her talking to you while you read! She has recorded numerous worship music projects, from prophetic books of the Bible, lullabies, instrumentals, prophetic flowing intercession, and beautiful worship CDs.

Harry and Cheryl are walking out the Lord's plan in their sessions of *School of Worship*. These are intensive training schools where the Salems teach, impart, and personally work with students to help them grow to the next level in their worship, life, and ministry.

Cheryl is founder and president of Women Of The Nation, an organization that is bringing together thousands of women who stand, pray and believe for this country. Under Cheryl's leadership these women are strategic, organized, unified and in prayer for our great nation. God gave Cheryl authority when she was crowned Miss America, and she is using that authority to stand in the gap for this great nation, for such a time as this!

Other books by Salem Family Ministries

Quips, Quotes, and Wisdom Notes

*Three Stages of Life

*Women of the Nation Pray!

*I Am A Worshiper

*I Am A Worshiper Workbook

*We Who Worship

*We Who Worship Workbook

*Rebuilding the Ruins of Worship

*Rebuilding the Ruins of Worship Workbook

*Tones of the Throne Room

*Tones of the Throne Room Workbook

*The Rise of an Orphan Generation: Longing for a Father

*Two Becoming One

*Don't Kill Each Other! Let God Do It!

*From Mourning to Morning

*From Grief to Glory

Distractions from Destiny

*Obtaining Peace - A 40-Day Prayer Journal

*Entering Rest - Be Still A 40-Day Prayer Journey

The Presence of Angels in Your Life

Overcoming Fear – A 40-Day Prayer Journal

*A Bright Shining Place - The Story of a Miracle

Speak the Word Over Your Family for Healing

Speak the Word Over Your Family for Finances

Speak the Word Over Your Family for Salvation

A Royal Child

The Mommy Book

Abuse . . . Bruised but not Broken

You Are Somebody

Choose to be Happy (out of print)

Health and Beauty Secrets (out of print)

Simple Facts: Salvation, Healing & the Holy Ghost (out of print)

Every Body Needs Balance (out of print)

The Choice is Yours (out of print)

Being #1 at Being #2 (out of print)

For Men Only (out of print)

It's Too Soon to Give Up (out of print)

Covenant Conquerors (out of print)

Warriors of the Word (out of print)

Fight in the Heavenlies (out of print)

Written by Dr. Harry Salem III

Grave Raiders

Feminine Spirits and Angels

Investigating Wonders

The Sound of the Spirit

Age of Mystery

Counting Ten Fingers for Patience Children's Book

Ten Shots for Do and Don't Children's Book

Ten Steps to Build and Be Spirit Filled Children's Book

Count of Ten Say Amen Children's Book

EBooks available at salemfamilyministries.org

Worship CDs and downloads are also available

If you would like more information about Salem Family Ministries, you can write to us or contact us via email on our website.

Salem Family Ministries
P. O. Box 1595
Cathedral City, CA 92235
www.salemfamilyministries.org

https://www.facebook.com/salemfamilyministries.org/

Subscribe to our YouTube channel Salem Family Ministries

Follow me on Instagram, CherylSalem1957

Printed in Great Britain
by Amazon

82111369R00108